Day Trading Log & Investing Journal

for active traders of stocks, options, futures, and forex

BY INCREDIBLY USEFUL NOTEBOOKS

Day Trading Log & Investing Journal
for active traders of stocks, options, futures, and forex
(day/intraday traders, binary traders, short-term traders, and investors)
Copyright © 2015 Incredibly Useful Notebooks

www.incrediblyusefulnotebooks.com

ISBN-13: 978-0692540107
ISBN-10: 0692540105

Day Trading Log & Investing Journal

for active traders of stocks, options, futures, and forex

BY INCREDIBLY USEFUL NOTEBOOKS

HOW TO USE THIS BOOK

Thank you for choosing one of our *Incredibly Useful Notebooks*. We have achieved a TRADING JOURNAL design that is both functional and intuitive for traders and investors of stocks, options, futures, and forex. This book is not meant to replace either the trade confirmations from your broker or any P/L (profit & loss) spreadsheets that you might use. Instead, this book is a written journal that helps you track your overall trades as you make them, with room for your thoughts and notes on market conditions, profit targets, stops, and more. With close tracking of your trading and investing plans comes refinement and better results. That's why we created this trading log.

Designed with the active stock, options, futures, and forex trader in mind, there is room on every page for either two separate sessions (morning and afternoon, for example), or two separate products, and a wide array of other uses. Busy traders might use a two-page spread as four time periods of a single trading day: overnight/pre-market (8-9:30AM EST), opening session (9:30-11AM EST), mid-day (11-1 PM EST), and the closing session (1-4PM EST), for example.

This design is intended to be useful for intraday and short-term traders, as well as longer-term use by swing traders, and for critical monthly/quarterly/annual trading review. The simple act of writing down each trade chronicles the decision-making process of each trader. Many traders believe that written trading logs and journals like this increase one's overall emotional control of the "fear vs. greed" balance at play in every market.

DATE:

Use any calendar date format that you prefer (MM/DD/YYYY), or just use the month and day.

MARKET CONDITIONS:

This box is where you make note of the overall market based on your trading parameters. If you're trading stocks, you might write down quotes of the SPY, QQQ, DIA, or IWM when you make your trade. Many traders like to use the S&P500 E-mini /ES futures to gauge current market activity. You might also regularly track oil, gold, volatility (VIX), the US dollar (USD), the Japanese yen (JPY), or the euro (EUR) as either exchange traded funds or in the futures market. If you trade commodities, you might regularly track silver, platinum, corn, sugar, coffee, natural gas, and more.

This record of 'context' is a key aspect of the journal because trade confirmations from your broker don't often contain overall market information at the time of the trade.

Stock Market: SPY, QQQ, DIA, IWM, /ES, /NQ, /YM, /TF
Currencies: EUR/USD, USD/JPY, GBP/USD, /6E, /6J
Commodities: DBA, USO, GLD, /CL, /GC, /NG, /ZC, /ZS
Volatility: VIX, /VX, UVXY, VXX

HOW TO USE THIS BOOK

The market conditions box has room for more than one indicator, but the design concept was to provide room for the one or two reference holdings or indexes specifically related to the trade below. For example, if you're day trading a technology stock, you might just write down the quote of the QQQ and the /NQ, at the time of the trade. If you're trading an oil services company, you might note the /ES, the USO, and /CL, to give a snapshot of the market and the price of light sweet crude. This section is followed by simple check boxes for STOCKS, OPTIONS, FUTURES, and FOREX, to identify all of your trades quickly.

AVAILABLE FUNDS:

The simplest way to use this section is to log your available trading capital at the beginning of your session. The extra room in the box gives you space to note the full value of your account ('net liquidation' amount), and an intraday buying power (or margin) amount. It's also possible to list two accounts (trading portfolio and retirement funds), or two balance limits (options buying power, and stock buying power), for example.

TRADING BOX:

In this area, you can mark the buy or sell time, quantity, and the name and symbol for each stock, option, future, or forex trade. Feel free to use BTO/STO (buy or sell to open) and BTC/STC (buy or sell to close) if that makes sense with your trading. The PRICE is the executed price, and the COST is the total amount you paid. For example, buying 500 shares of stock with a PRICE of $10, the total COST is calculated as 500 shares x $10.00 plus your transaction fees, or possibly $5,007.99. If you sell it later, you can create a new TIME, QUANTITY, and PRICE. With this example, imagine that you sold your holding at a PRICE of $10.27. For proceeds, you can use 500 shares x $10.27 minus your transaction fees, or, in this case, $5,127.01. In NET GAIN, you calculate the difference between PROCEEDS and COST as your NET GAIN or (LOSS). In our example, $5,127.01 minus $5,007.99 equals an overall net gain of $119.02. A column to track PERCENTAGE gain is also provided.

TARGET/STOP:

In this area, you can mark your trade stops (if applicable), and profit targets. For traders who don't use stops, short and medium-term support and resistance levels can be entered here.

ROI/ROR/ROC:

This box is for trade evaluation depending on your individual needs: return on investment (R.O.I.), return on risk (R.O.R.), or return on capital (R.O.C.) can be tracked here.

NOTES:

Use this box to note any trade-related comments, explain your reasons for taking the trade (high implied volatility, candlestick charts, etc.), and/or how you discovered the trade (watch lists, screeners, etc.).

Also, this *Day Trading Log & Investing Journal* features additional pages for your trading plans, strategies, goals, and trading rules. After the trade pages, you'll also find some open four-column tracking pages and lined note pages. Use these for weekly/monthly summaries, and performance tracking (win/loss ratios, average/max winning and losing trades, overall R.O.C., R.O.R., or R.O.I.), or anything else that fits your individual needs.

◊◊◊

TRADING PLAN/STRATEGY

DATE:

DATE:

INVESTMENT PLAN

DATE:

GOALS

DATE:

TRADING RULES

DATE:

DATE | MARKET CONDITIONS:

STOCKS ○   OPTIONS ○   FUTURES ○   FOREX ○   AVAILABLE FUNDS ($,¥,£,€):

Time	Buy Sell	Quantity	Name/Symbol	Price	Cost	Proceeds	Net Gain (Loss)	%

TARGET / STOP: | R.O.I./R.O.R./R.O.C.:

NOTES

· ·

DATE | MARKET CONDITIONS:

STOCKS ○   OPTIONS ○   FUTURES ○   FOREX ○   AVAILABLE FUNDS ($,¥,£,€):

Time	Buy Sell	Quantity	Name/Symbol	Price	Cost	Proceeds	Net Gain (Loss)	%

TARGET / STOP: | R.O.I./R.O.R./R.O.C.:

NOTES

DATE | MARKET CONDITIONS:

STOCKS ◯   OPTIONS ◯   FUTURES ◯   FOREX ◯   AVAILABLE FUNDS ($,¥,£,€):

Time	Buy Sell	Quantity	Name/Symbol	Price	Cost	Proceeds	Net Gain (Loss)	%

TARGET / STOP: | R.O.I./R.O.R./R.O.C.:

NOTES

• •

DATE | MARKET CONDITIONS:

STOCKS ◯   OPTIONS ◯   FUTURES ◯   FOREX ◯   AVAILABLE FUNDS ($,¥,£,€):

Time	Buy Sell	Quantity	Name/Symbol	Price	Cost	Proceeds	Net Gain (Loss)	%

TARGET / STOP: | R.O.I./R.O.R./R.O.C.:

NOTES

DATE

MARKET CONDITIONS:

STOCKS ○ OPTIONS ○ FUTURES ○ FOREX ○   AVAILABLE FUNDS ($,¥,£,€):

Time	Buy Sell	Quantity	Name/Symbol	Price	Cost	Proceeds	Net Gain (Loss)	%

TARGET / STOP: R.O.I./R.O.R./R.O.C.:

NOTES

· ·

DATE

MARKET CONDITIONS:

STOCKS ○ OPTIONS ○ FUTURES ○ FOREX ○   AVAILABLE FUNDS ($,¥,£,€):

Time	Buy Sell	Quantity	Name/Symbol	Price	Cost	Proceeds	Net Gain (Loss)	%

TARGET / STOP: R.O.I./R.O.R./R.O.C.:

NOTES

DATE

MARKET CONDITIONS:

STOCKS ○ OPTIONS ○ FUTURES ○ FOREX ○

AVAILABLE FUNDS ($,¥,£,€):

Time	Buy Sell	Quantity	Name/Symbol	Price	Cost	Proceeds	Net Gain (Loss)	%

TARGET / STOP:

R.O.I./R.O.R./R.O.C.:

NOTES

• •

DATE

MARKET CONDITIONS:

STOCKS ○ OPTIONS ○ FUTURES ○ FOREX ○

AVAILABLE FUNDS ($,¥,£,€):

Time	Buy Sell	Quantity	Name/Symbol	Price	Cost	Proceeds	Net Gain (Loss)	%

TARGET / STOP:

R.O.I./R.O.R./R.O.C.:

NOTES

DATE	MARKET CONDITIONS:						

STOCKS ○   OPTIONS ○   FUTURES ○   FOREX ○

AVAILABLE FUNDS ($,¥,£,€):

Time	Buy Sell	Quantity	Name/Symbol	Price	Cost	Proceeds	Net Gain (Loss)	%

TARGET / STOP: R.O.I./R.O.R./R.O.C.:

NOTES

· ·

DATE	MARKET CONDITIONS:						

STOCKS ○   OPTIONS ○   FUTURES ○   FOREX ○

AVAILABLE FUNDS ($,¥,£,€):

Time	Buy Sell	Quantity	Name/Symbol	Price	Cost	Proceeds	Net Gain (Loss)	%

TARGET / STOP: R.O.I./R.O.R./R.O.C.:

NOTES

DATE

MARKET CONDITIONS:

STOCKS ○   OPTIONS ○   FUTURES ○   FOREX ○   AVAILABLE FUNDS ($,¥,£,€):

Time	Buy Sell	Quantity	Name/Symbol	Price	Cost	Proceeds	Net Gain (Loss)	%

TARGET / STOP:

R.O.I./R.O.R./R.O.C.:

NOTES

· ·

DATE

MARKET CONDITIONS:

STOCKS ○   OPTIONS ○   FUTURES ○   FOREX ○   AVAILABLE FUNDS ($,¥,£,€):

Time	Buy Sell	Quantity	Name/Symbol	Price	Cost	Proceeds	Net Gain (Loss)	%

TARGET / STOP:

R.O.I./R.O.R./R.O.C.:

NOTES

DATE

MARKET CONDITIONS:

STOCKS ◯   OPTIONS ◯   FUTURES ◯   FOREX ◯

AVAILABLE FUNDS ($,¥,£,€):

Time	Buy Sell	Quantity	Name/Symbol	Price	Cost	Proceeds	Net Gain (Loss)	%

TARGET / STOP:

R.O.I./R.O.R./R.O.C.:

NOTES

· ·

DATE

MARKET CONDITIONS:

STOCKS ◯   OPTIONS ◯   FUTURES ◯   FOREX ◯

AVAILABLE FUNDS ($,¥,£,€):

Time	Buy Sell	Quantity	Name/Symbol	Price	Cost	Proceeds	Net Gain (Loss)	%

TARGET / STOP:

R.O.I./R.O.R./R.O.C.:

NOTES

DATE

MARKET CONDITIONS:

STOCKS ◯ OPTIONS ◯ FUTURES ◯ FOREX ◯

AVAILABLE FUNDS ($,¥,£,€):

Time	Buy Sell	Quantity	Name/Symbol	Price	Cost	Proceeds	Net Gain (Loss)	%

TARGET / STOP:

R.O.I./R.O.R./R.O.C.:

NOTES

- -

DATE

MARKET CONDITIONS:

STOCKS ◯ OPTIONS ◯ FUTURES ◯ FOREX ◯

AVAILABLE FUNDS ($,¥,£,€):

Time	Buy Sell	Quantity	Name/Symbol	Price	Cost	Proceeds	Net Gain (Loss)	%

TARGET / STOP:

R.O.I./R.O.R./R.O.C.:

NOTES

DATE
MARKET CONDITIONS:

STOCKS ○ OPTIONS ○ FUTURES ○ FOREX ○ AVAILABLE FUNDS ($,¥,£,€):

Time	Buy Sell	Quantity	Name/Symbol	Price	Cost	Proceeds	Net Gain (Loss)	%

TARGET / STOP: R.O.I./R.O.R./R.O.C.:

NOTES

- -

DATE
MARKET CONDITIONS:

STOCKS ○ OPTIONS ○ FUTURES ○ FOREX ○ AVAILABLE FUNDS ($,¥,£,€):

Time	Buy Sell	Quantity	Name/Symbol	Price	Cost	Proceeds	Net Gain (Loss)	%

TARGET / STOP: R.O.I./R.O.R./R.O.C.:

NOTES

DATE

MARKET CONDITIONS:

STOCKS ○   OPTIONS ○   FUTURES ○   FOREX ○

AVAILABLE FUNDS ($,¥,£,€):

Time	Buy Sell	Quantity	Name/Symbol	Price	Cost	Proceeds	Net Gain (Loss)	%

TARGET / STOP:

R.O.I./R.O.R./R.O.C.:

NOTES

DATE

MARKET CONDITIONS:

STOCKS ○   OPTIONS ○   FUTURES ○   FOREX ○

AVAILABLE FUNDS ($,¥,£,€):

Time	Buy Sell	Quantity	Name/Symbol	Price	Cost	Proceeds	Net Gain (Loss)	%

TARGET / STOP:

R.O.I./R.O.R./R.O.C.:

NOTES

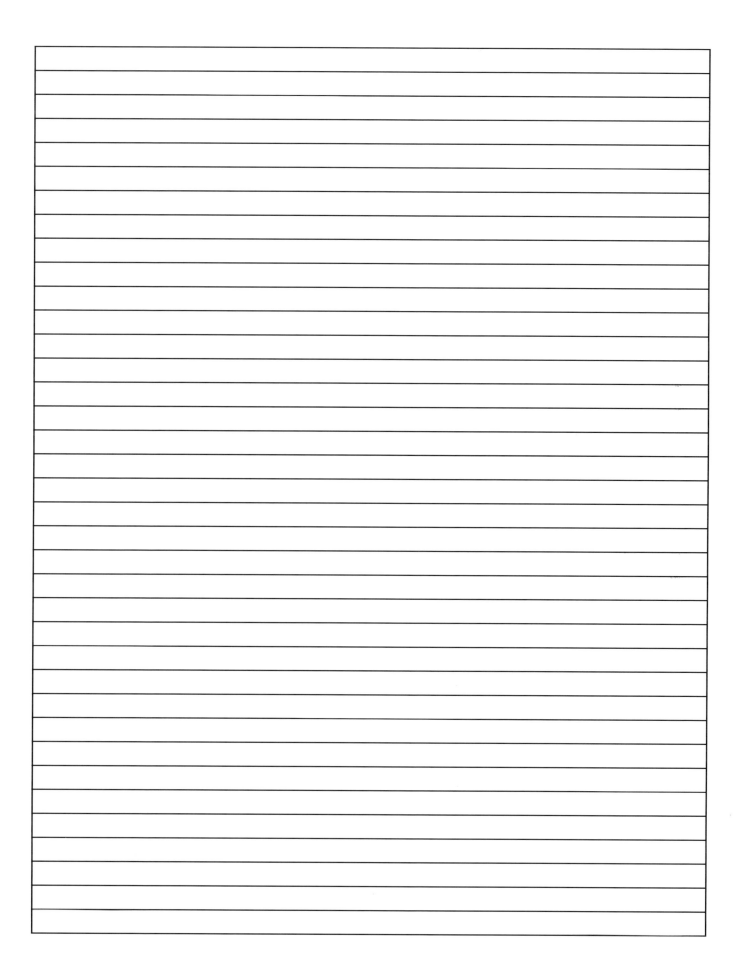

DATE

MARKET CONDITIONS:

STOCKS ◯   OPTIONS ◯   FUTURES ◯   FOREX ◯   AVAILABLE FUNDS ($,¥,£,€):

Time	Buy Sell	Quantity	Name/Symbol	Price	Cost	Proceeds	Net Gain (Loss)	%

TARGET / STOP:

R.O.I./R.O.R./R.O.C.:

NOTES

· ·

DATE

MARKET CONDITIONS:

STOCKS ◯   OPTIONS ◯   FUTURES ◯   FOREX ◯   AVAILABLE FUNDS ($,¥,£,€):

Time	Buy Sell	Quantity	Name/Symbol	Price	Cost	Proceeds	Net Gain (Loss)	%

TARGET / STOP:

R.O.I./R.O.R./R.O.C.:

NOTES

DATE

MARKET CONDITIONS:

STOCKS ○ OPTIONS ○ FUTURES ○ FOREX ○

AVAILABLE FUNDS ($,¥,£,€):

Time	Buy Sell	Quantity	Name/Symbol	Price	Cost	Proceeds	Net Gain (Loss)	%

TARGET / STOP:

R.O.I./R.O.R./R.O.C.:

NOTES

- -

DATE

MARKET CONDITIONS:

STOCKS ○ OPTIONS ○ FUTURES ○ FOREX ○

AVAILABLE FUNDS ($,¥,£,€):

Time	Buy Sell	Quantity	Name/Symbol	Price	Cost	Proceeds	Net Gain (Loss)	%

TARGET / STOP:

R.O.I./R.O.R./R.O.C.:

NOTES

DATE _____ MARKET CONDITIONS: _____

STOCKS ○   OPTIONS ○   FUTURES ○   FOREX ○   AVAILABLE FUNDS ($,¥,£,€): _____

Time	Buy Sell	Quantity	Name/Symbol	Price	Cost	Proceeds	Net Gain (Loss)	%

TARGET / STOP: _____   R.O.I./R.O.R./R.O.C.: _____

NOTES _____

- -

DATE _____ MARKET CONDITIONS: _____

STOCKS ○   OPTIONS ○   FUTURES ○   FOREX ○   AVAILABLE FUNDS ($,¥,£,€): _____

Time	Buy Sell	Quantity	Name/Symbol	Price	Cost	Proceeds	Net Gain (Loss)	%

TARGET / STOP: _____   R.O.I./R.O.R./R.O.C.: _____

NOTES _____

DATE	MARKET CONDITIONS:

STOCKS ○   OPTIONS ○   FUTURES ○   FOREX ○   AVAILABLE FUNDS ($,¥,£,€):

Time	Buy Sell	Quantity	Name/Symbol	Price	Cost	Proceeds	Net Gain (Loss)	%

TARGET / STOP:	R.O.I./R.O.R./R.O.C.:

NOTES

• •

DATE	MARKET CONDITIONS:

STOCKS ○   OPTIONS ○   FUTURES ○   FOREX ○   AVAILABLE FUNDS ($,¥,£,€):

Time	Buy Sell	Quantity	Name/Symbol	Price	Cost	Proceeds	Net Gain (Loss)	%

TARGET / STOP:	R.O.I./R.O.R./R.O.C.:

NOTES

DATE

MARKET CONDITIONS:

STOCKS ☐ OPTIONS ☐ FUTURES ☐ FOREX ☐

AVAILABLE FUNDS ($,¥,£,€):

Time	Buy Sell	Quantity	Name/Symbol	Price	Cost	Proceeds	Net Gain (Loss)	%

TARGET / STOP:

R.O.I./R.O.R./R.O.C.:

NOTES

· ·

DATE

MARKET CONDITIONS:

STOCKS ☐ OPTIONS ☐ FUTURES ☐ FOREX ☐

AVAILABLE FUNDS ($,¥,£,€):

Time	Buy Sell	Quantity	Name/Symbol	Price	Cost	Proceeds	Net Gain (Loss)	%

TARGET / STOP:

R.O.I./R.O.R./R.O.C.:

NOTES

DATE

MARKET CONDITIONS:

STOCKS ◯   OPTIONS ◯   FUTURES ◯   FOREX ◯

AVAILABLE FUNDS ($,¥,£,€):

Time	Buy Sell	Quantity	Name/Symbol	Price	Cost	Proceeds	Net Gain (Loss)	%

TARGET / STOP:

R.O.I./R.O.R./R.O.C.:

NOTES

• •

DATE

MARKET CONDITIONS:

STOCKS ◯   OPTIONS ◯   FUTURES ◯   FOREX ◯

AVAILABLE FUNDS ($,¥,£,€):

Time	Buy Sell	Quantity	Name/Symbol	Price	Cost	Proceeds	Net Gain (Loss)	%

TARGET / STOP:

R.O.I./R.O.R./R.O.C.:

NOTES

DATE | MARKET CONDITIONS:

STOCKS ◯ OPTIONS ◯ FUTURES ◯ FOREX ◯ AVAILABLE FUNDS ($,¥,£,€):

Time	Buy Sell	Quantity	Name/Symbol	Price	Cost	Proceeds	Net Gain (Loss)	%

TARGET / STOP: | R.O.I./R.O.R./R.O.C.:

NOTES

· ·

DATE | MARKET CONDITIONS:

STOCKS ◯ OPTIONS ◯ FUTURES ◯ FOREX ◯ AVAILABLE FUNDS ($,¥,£,€):

Time	Buy Sell	Quantity	Name/Symbol	Price	Cost	Proceeds	Net Gain (Loss)	%

TARGET / STOP: | R.O.I./R.O.R./R.O.C.:

NOTES

DATE

MARKET CONDITIONS:

STOCKS ◯   OPTIONS ◯   FUTURES ◯   FOREX ◯   AVAILABLE FUNDS ($,¥,£,€):

Time	Buy Sell	Quantity	Name/Symbol	Price	Cost	Proceeds	Net Gain (Loss)	%

TARGET / STOP: R.O.I./R.O.R./R.O.C.:

NOTES

DATE

MARKET CONDITIONS:

STOCKS ◯   OPTIONS ◯   FUTURES ◯   FOREX ◯   AVAILABLE FUNDS ($,¥,£,€):

Time	Buy Sell	Quantity	Name/Symbol	Price	Cost	Proceeds	Net Gain (Loss)	%

TARGET / STOP: R.O.I./R.O.R./R.O.C.:

NOTES

DATE

MARKET CONDITIONS:

STOCKS ◯ OPTIONS ◯ FUTURES ◯ FOREX ◯

AVAILABLE FUNDS ($,¥,£,€):

Time	Buy Sell	Quantity	Name/Symbol	Price	Cost	Proceeds	Net Gain (Loss)	%

TARGET / STOP:

R.O.I./R.O.R./R.O.C.:

NOTES

· ·

DATE

MARKET CONDITIONS:

STOCKS ◯ OPTIONS ◯ FUTURES ◯ FOREX ◯

AVAILABLE FUNDS ($,¥,£,€):

Time	Buy Sell	Quantity	Name/Symbol	Price	Cost	Proceeds	Net Gain (Loss)	%

TARGET / STOP:

R.O.I./R.O.R./R.O.C.:

NOTES

DATE

MARKET CONDITIONS:

STOCKS ◯ OPTIONS ◯ FUTURES ◯ FOREX ◯ AVAILABLE FUNDS ($,¥,£,€):

Time	Buy Sell	Quantity	Name/Symbol	Price	Cost	Proceeds	Net Gain (Loss)	%

TARGET / STOP:

R.O.I./R.O.R./R.O.C.:

NOTES

• •

DATE

MARKET CONDITIONS:

STOCKS ◯ OPTIONS ◯ FUTURES ◯ FOREX ◯ AVAILABLE FUNDS ($,¥,£,€):

Time	Buy Sell	Quantity	Name/Symbol	Price	Cost	Proceeds	Net Gain (Loss)	%

TARGET / STOP:

R.O.I./R.O.R./R.O.C.:

NOTES

DATE

MARKET CONDITIONS:

STOCKS ○ OPTIONS ○ FUTURES ○ FOREX ○

AVAILABLE FUNDS ($,¥,£,€):

Time	Buy Sell	Quantity	Name/Symbol	Price	Cost	Proceeds	Net Gain (Loss)	%

TARGET / STOP:

R.O.I./R.O.R./R.O.C.:

NOTES

- -

DATE

MARKET CONDITIONS:

STOCKS ○ OPTIONS ○ FUTURES ○ FOREX ○

AVAILABLE FUNDS ($,¥,£,€):

Time	Buy Sell	Quantity	Name/Symbol	Price	Cost	Proceeds	Net Gain (Loss)	%

TARGET / STOP:

R.O.I./R.O.R./R.O.C.:

NOTES

DATE

MARKET CONDITIONS:

STOCKS ◯ OPTIONS ◯ FUTURES ◯ FOREX ◯ AVAILABLE FUNDS ($,¥,£,€):

Time	Buy Sell	Quantity	Name/Symbol	Price	Cost	Proceeds	Net Gain (Loss)	%

TARGET / STOP:

R.O.I./R.O.R./R.O.C.:

NOTES

· ·

DATE

MARKET CONDITIONS:

STOCKS ◯ OPTIONS ◯ FUTURES ◯ FOREX ◯ AVAILABLE FUNDS ($,¥,£,€):

Time	Buy Sell	Quantity	Name/Symbol	Price	Cost	Proceeds	Net Gain (Loss)	%

TARGET / STOP:

R.O.I./R.O.R./R.O.C.:

NOTES

DATE

MARKET CONDITIONS:

STOCKS ◯ OPTIONS ◯ FUTURES ◯ FOREX ◯

AVAILABLE FUNDS ($,¥,£,€):

Time	Buy Sell	Quantity	Name/Symbol	Price	Cost	Proceeds	Net Gain (Loss)	%

TARGET / STOP:

R.O.I./R.O.R./R.O.C.:

NOTES

· ·

DATE

MARKET CONDITIONS:

STOCKS ◯ OPTIONS ◯ FUTURES ◯ FOREX ◯

AVAILABLE FUNDS ($,¥,£,€):

Time	Buy Sell	Quantity	Name/Symbol	Price	Cost	Proceeds	Net Gain (Loss)	%

TARGET / STOP:

R.O.I./R.O.R./R.O.C.:

NOTES

DATE

MARKET CONDITIONS:

STOCKS ⚪ OPTIONS ⚪ FUTURES ⚪ FOREX ⚪

AVAILABLE FUNDS ($,¥,£,€):

Time	Buy Sell	Quantity	Name/Symbol	Price	Cost	Proceeds	Net Gain (Loss)	%

TARGET / STOP:

R.O.I./R.O.R./R.O.C.:

NOTES

DATE

MARKET CONDITIONS:

STOCKS ⚪ OPTIONS ⚪ FUTURES ⚪ FOREX ⚪

AVAILABLE FUNDS ($,¥,£,€):

Time	Buy Sell	Quantity	Name/Symbol	Price	Cost	Proceeds	Net Gain (Loss)	%

TARGET / STOP:

R.O.I./R.O.R./R.O.C.:

NOTES

DATE

MARKET CONDITIONS:

STOCKS ☐ OPTIONS ☐ FUTURES ☐ FOREX ☐ AVAILABLE FUNDS ($,¥,£,€):

Time	Buy Sell	Quantity	Name/Symbol	Price	Cost	Proceeds	Net Gain (Loss)	%

TARGET / STOP: R.O.I./R.O.R./R.O.C.:

NOTES

. . . .

DATE

MARKET CONDITIONS:

STOCKS ☐ OPTIONS ☐ FUTURES ☐ FOREX ☐ AVAILABLE FUNDS ($,¥,£,€):

Time	Buy Sell	Quantity	Name/Symbol	Price	Cost	Proceeds	Net Gain (Loss)	%

TARGET / STOP: R.O.I./R.O.R./R.O.C.:

NOTES

DATE

MARKET CONDITIONS:

STOCKS ○   OPTIONS ○   FUTURES ○   FOREX ○

AVAILABLE FUNDS ($,¥,£,€):

Time	Buy Sell	Quantity	Name/Symbol	Price	Cost	Proceeds	Net Gain (Loss)	%

TARGET / STOP:

R.O.I./R.O.R./R.O.C.:

NOTES

- -

DATE

MARKET CONDITIONS:

STOCKS ○   OPTIONS ○   FUTURES ○   FOREX ○

AVAILABLE FUNDS ($,¥,£,€):

Time	Buy Sell	Quantity	Name/Symbol	Price	Cost	Proceeds	Net Gain (Loss)	%

TARGET / STOP:

R.O.I./R.O.R./R.O.C.:

NOTES

DATE

MARKET CONDITIONS:

STOCKS ◯   OPTIONS ◯   FUTURES ◯   FOREX ◯   AVAILABLE FUNDS ($,¥,£,€):

Time	Buy Sell	Quantity	Name/Symbol	Price	Cost	Proceeds	Net Gain (Loss)	%

TARGET / STOP: R.O.I./R.O.R./R.O.C.:

NOTES

• •

DATE

MARKET CONDITIONS:

STOCKS ◯   OPTIONS ◯   FUTURES ◯   FOREX ◯   AVAILABLE FUNDS ($,¥,£,€):

Time	Buy Sell	Quantity	Name/Symbol	Price	Cost	Proceeds	Net Gain (Loss)	%

TARGET / STOP: R.O.I./R.O.R./R.O.C.:

NOTES

DATE	MARKET CONDITIONS:

STOCKS ○   OPTIONS ○   FUTURES ○   FOREX ○ | AVAILABLE FUNDS ($,¥,£,€): |

Time	Buy Sell	Quantity	Name/Symbol	Price	Cost	Proceeds	Net Gain (Loss)	%

TARGET / STOP:	R.O.I./R.O.R./R.O.C.:

NOTES

- -

DATE	MARKET CONDITIONS:

STOCKS ○   OPTIONS ○   FUTURES ○   FOREX ○ | AVAILABLE FUNDS ($,¥,£,€): |

Time	Buy Sell	Quantity	Name/Symbol	Price	Cost	Proceeds	Net Gain (Loss)	%

TARGET / STOP:	R.O.I./R.O.R./R.O.C.:

NOTES

DATE

MARKET CONDITIONS:

STOCKS ○ OPTIONS ○ FUTURES ○ FOREX ○

AVAILABLE FUNDS ($,¥,£,€):

Time	Buy Sell	Quantity	Name/Symbol	Price	Cost	Proceeds	Net Gain (Loss)	%

TARGET / STOP:

R.O.I./R.O.R./R.O.C.:

NOTES

....

DATE

MARKET CONDITIONS:

STOCKS ○ OPTIONS ○ FUTURES ○ FOREX ○

AVAILABLE FUNDS ($,¥,£,€):

Time	Buy Sell	Quantity	Name/Symbol	Price	Cost	Proceeds	Net Gain (Loss)	%

TARGET / STOP:

R.O.I./R.O.R./R.O.C.:

NOTES

DATE

MARKET CONDITIONS:

STOCKS ○ OPTIONS ○ FUTURES ○ FOREX ○

AVAILABLE FUNDS ($,¥,£,€):

Time	Buy Sell	Quantity	Name/Symbol	Price	Cost	Proceeds	Net Gain (Loss)	%

TARGET / STOP:

R.O.I./R.O.R./R.O.C.:

NOTES

- -

DATE

MARKET CONDITIONS:

STOCKS ○ OPTIONS ○ FUTURES ○ FOREX ○

AVAILABLE FUNDS ($,¥,£,€):

Time	Buy Sell	Quantity	Name/Symbol	Price	Cost	Proceeds	Net Gain (Loss)	%

TARGET / STOP:

R.O.I./R.O.R./R.O.C.:

NOTES

DATE

MARKET CONDITIONS:

STOCKS ○ OPTIONS ○ FUTURES ○ FOREX ○ AVAILABLE FUNDS ($,¥,£,€):

Time	Buy Sell	Quantity	Name/Symbol	Price	Cost	Proceeds	Net Gain (Loss)	%

TARGET / STOP:

R.O.I./R.O.R./R.O.C.:

NOTES

• •

DATE

MARKET CONDITIONS:

STOCKS ○ OPTIONS ○ FUTURES ○ FOREX ○ AVAILABLE FUNDS ($,¥,£,€):

Time	Buy Sell	Quantity	Name/Symbol	Price	Cost	Proceeds	Net Gain (Loss)	%

TARGET / STOP:

R.O.I./R.O.R./R.O.C.:

NOTES

DATE

MARKET CONDITIONS:

STOCKS ⭘ OPTIONS ⭘ FUTURES ⭘ FOREX ⭘   AVAILABLE FUNDS ($,¥,£,€):

Time	Buy Sell	Quantity	Name/Symbol	Price	Cost	Proceeds	Net Gain (Loss)	%

TARGET / STOP: R.O.I./R.O.R./R.O.C.:

NOTES

DATE

MARKET CONDITIONS:

STOCKS ⭘ OPTIONS ⭘ FUTURES ⭘ FOREX ⭘   AVAILABLE FUNDS ($,¥,£,€):

Time	Buy Sell	Quantity	Name/Symbol	Price	Cost	Proceeds	Net Gain (Loss)	%

TARGET / STOP: R.O.I./R.O.R./R.O.C.:

NOTES

MARKET CONDITIONS:

STOCKS ○ OPTIONS ○ FUTURES ○ FOREX ○

AVAILABLE FUNDS ($,¥,£,€):

Time	Buy Sell	Quantity	Name/Symbol	Price	Cost	Proceeds	Net Gain (Loss)	%

TARGET / STOP:

R.O.I./R.O.R./R.O.C.:

NOTES

· ·

MARKET CONDITIONS:

STOCKS ○ OPTIONS ○ FUTURES ○ FOREX ○

AVAILABLE FUNDS ($,¥,£,€):

Time	Buy Sell	Quantity	Name/Symbol	Price	Cost	Proceeds	Net Gain (Loss)	%

TARGET / STOP:

R.O.I./R.O.R./R.O.C.:

NOTES

DATE

MARKET CONDITIONS:

STOCKS ○   OPTIONS ○   FUTURES ○   FOREX ○   AVAILABLE FUNDS ($,¥,£,€):

Time	Buy Sell	Quantity	Name/Symbol	Price	Cost	Proceeds	Net Gain (Loss)	%

TARGET / STOP: R.O.I./R.O.R./R.O.C.:

NOTES

· ·

DATE

MARKET CONDITIONS:

STOCKS ○   OPTIONS ○   FUTURES ○   FOREX ○   AVAILABLE FUNDS ($,¥,£,€):

Time	Buy Sell	Quantity	Name/Symbol	Price	Cost	Proceeds	Net Gain (Loss)	%

TARGET / STOP: R.O.I./R.O.R./R.O.C.:

NOTES

DATE

MARKET CONDITIONS:

STOCKS ◯ OPTIONS ◯ FUTURES ◯ FOREX ◯

AVAILABLE FUNDS ($,¥,£,€):

Time	Buy Sell	Quantity	Name/Symbol	Price	Cost	Proceeds	Net Gain (Loss)	%

TARGET / STOP:

R.O.I./R.O.R./R.O.C.:

NOTES

· ·

DATE

MARKET CONDITIONS:

STOCKS ◯ OPTIONS ◯ FUTURES ◯ FOREX ◯

AVAILABLE FUNDS ($,¥,£,€):

Time	Buy Sell	Quantity	Name/Symbol	Price	Cost	Proceeds	Net Gain (Loss)	%

TARGET / STOP:

R.O.I./R.O.R./R.O.C.:

NOTES

DATE

MARKET CONDITIONS:

STOCKS ◯ OPTIONS ◯ FUTURES ◯ FOREX ◯

AVAILABLE FUNDS ($,¥,£,€):

Time	Buy Sell	Quantity	Name/Symbol	Price	Cost	Proceeds	Net Gain (Loss)	%

TARGET / STOP:

R.O.I./R.O.R./R.O.C.:

NOTES

· ·

DATE

MARKET CONDITIONS:

STOCKS ◯ OPTIONS ◯ FUTURES ◯ FOREX ◯

AVAILABLE FUNDS ($,¥,£,€):

Time	Buy Sell	Quantity	Name/Symbol	Price	Cost	Proceeds	Net Gain (Loss)	%

TARGET / STOP:

R.O.I./R.O.R./R.O.C.:

NOTES

DATE

MARKET CONDITIONS:

STOCKS ○   OPTIONS ○   FUTURES ○   FOREX ○

AVAILABLE FUNDS ($,¥,£,€):

Time	Buy Sell	Quantity	Name/Symbol	Price	Cost	Proceeds	Net Gain (Loss)	%

TARGET / STOP:

R.O.I./R.O.R./R.O.C.:

NOTES

· ·

DATE

MARKET CONDITIONS:

STOCKS ○   OPTIONS ○   FUTURES ○   FOREX ○

AVAILABLE FUNDS ($,¥,£,€):

Time	Buy Sell	Quantity	Name/Symbol	Price	Cost	Proceeds	Net Gain (Loss)	%

TARGET / STOP:

R.O.I./R.O.R./R.O.C.:

NOTES

DATE

MARKET CONDITIONS:

STOCKS ○ OPTIONS ○ FUTURES ○ FOREX ○

AVAILABLE FUNDS ($,¥,£,€):

Time	Buy Sell	Quantity	Name/Symbol	Price	Cost	Proceeds	Net Gain (Loss)	%

TARGET / STOP:

R.O.I./R.O.R./R.O.C.:

NOTES

DATE

MARKET CONDITIONS:

STOCKS ○ OPTIONS ○ FUTURES ○ FOREX ○

AVAILABLE FUNDS ($,¥,£,€):

Time	Buy Sell	Quantity	Name/Symbol	Price	Cost	Proceeds	Net Gain (Loss)	%

TARGET / STOP:

R.O.I./R.O.R./R.O.C.:

NOTES

DATE

MARKET CONDITIONS:

STOCKS ⃝ OPTIONS ⃝ FUTURES ⃝ FOREX ⃝

AVAILABLE FUNDS ($,¥,£,€):

Time	Buy Sell	Quantity	Name/Symbol	Price	Cost	Proceeds	Net Gain (Loss)	%

TARGET / STOP:

R.O.I./R.O.R./R.O.C.:

NOTES

· ·

DATE

MARKET CONDITIONS:

STOCKS ⃝ OPTIONS ⃝ FUTURES ⃝ FOREX ⃝

AVAILABLE FUNDS ($,¥,£,€):

Time	Buy Sell	Quantity	Name/Symbol	Price	Cost	Proceeds	Net Gain (Loss)	%

TARGET / STOP:

R.O.I./R.O.R./R.O.C.:

NOTES

MARKET CONDITIONS:

STOCKS ○ OPTIONS ○ FUTURES ○ FOREX ○ AVAILABLE FUNDS ($,¥,£,€):

Time	Buy Sell	Quantity	Name/Symbol	Price	Cost	Proceeds	Net Gain (Loss)	%

TARGET / STOP:

R.O.I./R.O.R./R.O.C.:

NOTES

· ·

DATE

MARKET CONDITIONS:

STOCKS ○ OPTIONS ○ FUTURES ○ FOREX ○ AVAILABLE FUNDS ($,¥,£,€):

Time	Buy Sell	Quantity	Name/Symbol	Price	Cost	Proceeds	Net Gain (Loss)	%

TARGET / STOP:

R.O.I./R.O.R./R.O.C.:

NOTES

DATE | MARKET CONDITIONS:

STOCKS ◯ OPTIONS ◯ FUTURES ◯ FOREX ◯ | AVAILABLE FUNDS ($,¥,£,€):

Time	Buy Sell	Quantity	Name/Symbol	Price	Cost	Proceeds	Net Gain (Loss)	%

TARGET / STOP: | R.O.I./R.O.R./R.O.C.:

NOTES

- -

DATE | MARKET CONDITIONS:

STOCKS ◯ OPTIONS ◯ FUTURES ◯ FOREX ◯ | AVAILABLE FUNDS ($,¥,£,€):

Time	Buy Sell	Quantity	Name/Symbol	Price	Cost	Proceeds	Net Gain (Loss)	%

TARGET / STOP: | R.O.I./R.O.R./R.O.C.:

NOTES

DATE

MARKET CONDITIONS:

STOCKS ○   OPTIONS ○   FUTURES ○   FOREX ○   AVAILABLE FUNDS ($,¥,£,€):

Time	Buy Sell	Quantity	Name/Symbol	Price	Cost	Proceeds	Net Gain (Loss)	%

TARGET / STOP: R.O.I./R.O.R./R.O.C.:

NOTES

DATE

MARKET CONDITIONS:

STOCKS ○   OPTIONS ○   FUTURES ○   FOREX ○   AVAILABLE FUNDS ($,¥,£,€):

Time	Buy Sell	Quantity	Name/Symbol	Price	Cost	Proceeds	Net Gain (Loss)	%

TARGET / STOP: R.O.I./R.O.R./R.O.C.:

NOTES

MARKET CONDITIONS:

STOCKS ◯ OPTIONS ◯ FUTURES ◯ FOREX ◯

AVAILABLE FUNDS ($,¥,£,€):

Time	Buy Sell	Quantity	Name/Symbol	Price	Cost	Proceeds	Net Gain (Loss)	%

TARGET / STOP:

R.O.I./R.O.R./R.O.C.:

NOTES

· ·

DATE

MARKET CONDITIONS:

STOCKS ◯ OPTIONS ◯ FUTURES ◯ FOREX ◯

AVAILABLE FUNDS ($,¥,£,€):

Time	Buy Sell	Quantity	Name/Symbol	Price	Cost	Proceeds	Net Gain (Loss)	%

TARGET / STOP:

R.O.I./R.O.R./R.O.C.:

NOTES

MARKET CONDITIONS:

STOCKS ○   OPTIONS ○   FUTURES ○   FOREX ○

AVAILABLE FUNDS ($,¥,£,€):

Time	Buy Sell	Quantity	Name/Symbol	Price	Cost	Proceeds	Net Gain (Loss)	%

TARGET / STOP:

R.O.I./R.O.R./R.O.C.:

NOTES

· ·

MARKET CONDITIONS:

STOCKS ○   OPTIONS ○   FUTURES ○   FOREX ○

AVAILABLE FUNDS ($,¥,£,€):

Time	Buy Sell	Quantity	Name/Symbol	Price	Cost	Proceeds	Net Gain (Loss)	%

TARGET / STOP:

R.O.I./R.O.R./R.O.C.:

NOTES

DATE

MARKET CONDITIONS:

STOCKS ◯ OPTIONS ◯ FUTURES ◯ FOREX ◯

AVAILABLE FUNDS ($,¥,£,€):

Time	Buy Sell	Quantity	Name/Symbol	Price	Cost	Proceeds	Net Gain (Loss)	%

TARGET / STOP:

R.O.I./R.O.R./R.O.C.:

NOTES

· ·

DATE

MARKET CONDITIONS:

STOCKS ◯ OPTIONS ◯ FUTURES ◯ FOREX ◯

AVAILABLE FUNDS ($,¥,£,€):

Time	Buy Sell	Quantity	Name/Symbol	Price	Cost	Proceeds	Net Gain (Loss)	%

TARGET / STOP:

R.O.I./R.O.R./R.O.C.:

NOTES

MARKET CONDITIONS:

STOCKS ○ OPTIONS ○ FUTURES ○ FOREX ○

AVAILABLE FUNDS ($,¥,£,€):

Time	Buy Sell	Quantity	Name/Symbol	Price	Cost	Proceeds	Net Gain (Loss)	%

TARGET / STOP:

R.O.I./R.O.R./R.O.C.:

NOTES

- -

DATE

MARKET CONDITIONS:

STOCKS ○ OPTIONS ○ FUTURES ○ FOREX ○

AVAILABLE FUNDS ($,¥,£,€):

Time	Buy Sell	Quantity	Name/Symbol	Price	Cost	Proceeds	Net Gain (Loss)	%

TARGET / STOP:

R.O.I./R.O.R./R.O.C.:

NOTES

DATE

MARKET CONDITIONS:

STOCKS ○   OPTIONS ○   FUTURES ○   FOREX ○

AVAILABLE FUNDS ($,¥,£,€):

Time	Buy Sell	Quantity	Name/Symbol	Price	Cost	Proceeds	Net Gain (Loss)	%

TARGET / STOP:

R.O.I./R.O.R./R.O.C.:

NOTES

· ·

DATE

MARKET CONDITIONS:

STOCKS ○   OPTIONS ○   FUTURES ○   FOREX ○

AVAILABLE FUNDS ($,¥,£,€):

Time	Buy Sell	Quantity	Name/Symbol	Price	Cost	Proceeds	Net Gain (Loss)	%

TARGET / STOP:

R.O.I./R.O.R./R.O.C.:

NOTES

DATE

MARKET CONDITIONS:

STOCKS ○   OPTIONS ○   FUTURES ○   FOREX ○

AVAILABLE FUNDS ($,¥,£,€):

Time	Buy Sell	Quantity	Name/Symbol	Price	Cost	Proceeds	Net Gain (Loss)	%

TARGET / STOP:

R.O.I./R.O.R./R.O.C.:

NOTES

- -

DATE

MARKET CONDITIONS:

STOCKS ○   OPTIONS ○   FUTURES ○   FOREX ○

AVAILABLE FUNDS ($,¥,£,€):

Time	Buy Sell	Quantity	Name/Symbol	Price	Cost	Proceeds	Net Gain (Loss)	%

TARGET / STOP:

R.O.I./R.O.R./R.O.C.:

NOTES

DATE

MARKET CONDITIONS:

STOCKS ○   OPTIONS ○   FUTURES ○   FOREX ○

AVAILABLE FUNDS ($,¥,£,€):

Time	Buy Sell	Quantity	Name/Symbol	Price	Cost	Proceeds	Net Gain (Loss)	%

TARGET / STOP:

R.O.I./R.O.R./R.O.C.:

NOTES

• •

DATE

MARKET CONDITIONS:

STOCKS ○   OPTIONS ○   FUTURES ○   FOREX ○

AVAILABLE FUNDS ($,¥,£,€):

Time	Buy Sell	Quantity	Name/Symbol	Price	Cost	Proceeds	Net Gain (Loss)	%

TARGET / STOP:

R.O.I./R.O.R./R.O.C.:

NOTES

DATE

MARKET CONDITIONS:

STOCKS OPTIONS FUTURES FOREX   AVAILABLE FUNDS ($,¥,£,€):
  ○   ○   ○   ○

Time	Buy Sell	Quantity	Name/Symbol	Price	Cost	Proceeds	Net Gain (Loss)	%

TARGET / STOP: R.O.I./R.O.R./R.O.C.:

NOTES

DATE

MARKET CONDITIONS:

STOCKS OPTIONS FUTURES FOREX   AVAILABLE FUNDS ($,¥,£,€):
  ○   ○   ○   ○

Time	Buy Sell	Quantity	Name/Symbol	Price	Cost	Proceeds	Net Gain (Loss)	%

TARGET / STOP: R.O.I./R.O.R./R.O.C.:

NOTES

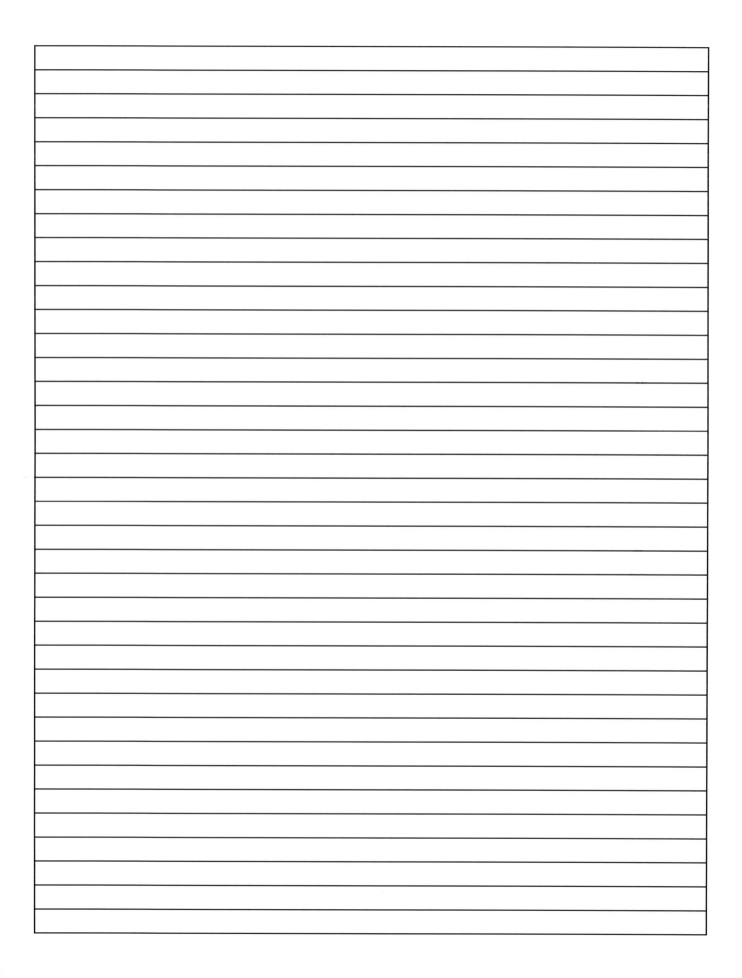

DATE

MARKET CONDITIONS:

STOCKS ○   OPTIONS ○   FUTURES ○   FOREX ○   AVAILABLE FUNDS ($,¥,£,€):

Time	Buy Sell	Quantity	Name/Symbol	Price	Cost	Proceeds	Net Gain (Loss)	%

TARGET / STOP: R.O.I./R.O.R./R.O.C.:

NOTES

. . . .

DATE

MARKET CONDITIONS:

STOCKS ○   OPTIONS ○   FUTURES ○   FOREX ○   AVAILABLE FUNDS ($,¥,£,€):

Time	Buy Sell	Quantity	Name/Symbol	Price	Cost	Proceeds	Net Gain (Loss)	%

TARGET / STOP: R.O.I./R.O.R./R.O.C.:

NOTES

MARKET CONDITIONS:

STOCKS ○   OPTIONS ○   FUTURES ○   FOREX ○

AVAILABLE FUNDS ($,¥,£,€):

Time	Buy Sell	Quantity	Name/Symbol	Price	Cost	Proceeds	Net Gain (Loss)	%

TARGET / STOP:

R.O.I./R.O.R./R.O.C.:

NOTES

• •

DATE

MARKET CONDITIONS:

STOCKS ○   OPTIONS ○   FUTURES ○   FOREX ○

AVAILABLE FUNDS ($,¥,£,€):

Time	Buy Sell	Quantity	Name/Symbol	Price	Cost	Proceeds	Net Gain (Loss)	%

TARGET / STOP:

R.O.I./R.O.R./R.O.C.:

NOTES

DATE

MARKET CONDITIONS:

STOCKS OPTIONS FUTURES FOREX AVAILABLE FUNDS ($,¥,£,€):
○   ○   ○   ○

Time	Buy Sell	Quantity	Name/Symbol	Price	Cost	Proceeds	Net Gain (Loss)	%

TARGET / STOP:

R.O.I./R.O.R./R.O.C.:

NOTES

DATE

MARKET CONDITIONS:

STOCKS OPTIONS FUTURES FOREX AVAILABLE FUNDS ($,¥,£,€):
○   ○   ○   ○

Time	Buy Sell	Quantity	Name/Symbol	Price	Cost	Proceeds	Net Gain (Loss)	%

TARGET / STOP:

R.O.I./R.O.R./R.O.C.:

NOTES

DATE

MARKET CONDITIONS:

STOCKS ○   OPTIONS ○   FUTURES ○   FOREX ○

AVAILABLE FUNDS ($,¥,£,€):

Time	Buy Sell	Quantity	Name/Symbol	Price	Cost	Proceeds	Net Gain (Loss)	%

TARGET / STOP:

R.O.I./R.O.R./R.O.C.:

NOTES

- -

DATE

MARKET CONDITIONS:

STOCKS ○   OPTIONS ○   FUTURES ○   FOREX ○

AVAILABLE FUNDS ($,¥,£,€):

Time	Buy Sell	Quantity	Name/Symbol	Price	Cost	Proceeds	Net Gain (Loss)	%

TARGET / STOP:

R.O.I./R.O.R./R.O.C.:

NOTES

DATE

MARKET CONDITIONS:

STOCKS ☐ OPTIONS ☐ FUTURES ☐ FOREX ☐

AVAILABLE FUNDS ($,¥,£,€):

Time	Buy Sell	Quantity	Name/Symbol	Price	Cost	Proceeds	Net Gain (Loss)	%

TARGET / STOP:

R.O.I./R.O.R./R.O.C.:

NOTES

• •

DATE

MARKET CONDITIONS:

STOCKS ☐ OPTIONS ☐ FUTURES ☐ FOREX ☐

AVAILABLE FUNDS ($,¥,£,€):

Time	Buy Sell	Quantity	Name/Symbol	Price	Cost	Proceeds	Net Gain (Loss)	%

TARGET / STOP:

R.O.I./R.O.R./R.O.C.:

NOTES

DATE

MARKET CONDITIONS:

STOCKS ○ OPTIONS ○ FUTURES ○ FOREX ○

AVAILABLE FUNDS ($,¥,£,€):

Time	Buy Sell	Quantity	Name/Symbol	Price	Cost	Proceeds	Net Gain (Loss)	%

TARGET / STOP:

R.O.I./R.O.R./R.O.C.:

NOTES

• •

DATE

MARKET CONDITIONS:

STOCKS ○ OPTIONS ○ FUTURES ○ FOREX ○

AVAILABLE FUNDS ($,¥,£,€):

Time	Buy Sell	Quantity	Name/Symbol	Price	Cost	Proceeds	Net Gain (Loss)	%

TARGET / STOP:

R.O.I./R.O.R./R.O.C.:

NOTES

DATE

MARKET CONDITIONS:

STOCKS ○　OPTIONS ○　FUTURES ○　FOREX ○

AVAILABLE FUNDS ($,¥,£,€):

Time	Buy Sell	Quantity	Name/Symbol	Price	Cost	Proceeds	Net Gain (Loss)	%

TARGET / STOP:

R.O.I./R.O.R./R.O.C.:

NOTES

· ·

DATE

MARKET CONDITIONS:

STOCKS ○　OPTIONS ○　FUTURES ○　FOREX ○

AVAILABLE FUNDS ($,¥,£,€):

Time	Buy Sell	Quantity	Name/Symbol	Price	Cost	Proceeds	Net Gain (Loss)	%

TARGET / STOP:

R.O.I./R.O.R./R.O.C.:

NOTES

MARKET CONDITIONS:

STOCKS ◯ OPTIONS ◯ FUTURES ◯ FOREX ◯   AVAILABLE FUNDS ($,¥,£,€):

Time	Buy Sell	Quantity	Name/Symbol	Price	Cost	Proceeds	Net Gain (Loss)	%

TARGET / STOP: R.O.I./R.O.R./R.O.C.:

NOTES

· ·

DATE

MARKET CONDITIONS:

STOCKS ◯ OPTIONS ◯ FUTURES ◯ FOREX ◯   AVAILABLE FUNDS ($,¥,£,€):

Time	Buy Sell	Quantity	Name/Symbol	Price	Cost	Proceeds	Net Gain (Loss)	%

TARGET / STOP: R.O.I./R.O.R./R.O.C.:

NOTES

| DATE | MARKET CONDITIONS: |

STOCKS ○ OPTIONS ○ FUTURES ○ FOREX ○ AVAILABLE FUNDS ($,¥,£,€):

Time	Buy Sell	Quantity	Name/Symbol	Price	Cost	Proceeds	Net Gain (Loss)	%

TARGET / STOP: R.O.I./R.O.R./R.O.C.:

NOTES

- -

| DATE | MARKET CONDITIONS: |

STOCKS ○ OPTIONS ○ FUTURES ○ FOREX ○ AVAILABLE FUNDS ($,¥,£,€):

Time	Buy Sell	Quantity	Name/Symbol	Price	Cost	Proceeds	Net Gain (Loss)	%

TARGET / STOP: R.O.I./R.O.R./R.O.C.:

NOTES

DATE

MARKET CONDITIONS:

STOCKS ◯ OPTIONS ◯ FUTURES ◯ FOREX ◯

AVAILABLE FUNDS ($,¥,£,€):

Time	Buy Sell	Quantity	Name/Symbol	Price	Cost	Proceeds	Net Gain (Loss)	%

TARGET / STOP:

R.O.I./R.O.R./R.O.C.:

NOTES

• •

DATE

MARKET CONDITIONS:

STOCKS ◯ OPTIONS ◯ FUTURES ◯ FOREX ◯

AVAILABLE FUNDS ($,¥,£,€):

Time	Buy Sell	Quantity	Name/Symbol	Price	Cost	Proceeds	Net Gain (Loss)	%

TARGET / STOP:

R.O.I./R.O.R./R.O.C.:

NOTES

DATE

MARKET CONDITIONS:

STOCKS ◯ OPTIONS ◯ FUTURES ◯ FOREX ◯

AVAILABLE FUNDS ($,¥,£,€):

Time	Buy Sell	Quantity	Name/Symbol	Price	Cost	Proceeds	Net Gain (Loss)	%

TARGET / STOP:

R.O.I./R.O.R./R.O.C.:

NOTES

- -

DATE

MARKET CONDITIONS:

STOCKS ◯ OPTIONS ◯ FUTURES ◯ FOREX ◯

AVAILABLE FUNDS ($,¥,£,€):

Time	Buy Sell	Quantity	Name/Symbol	Price	Cost	Proceeds	Net Gain (Loss)	%

TARGET / STOP:

R.O.I./R.O.R./R.O.C.:

NOTES

DATE | MARKET CONDITIONS:

STOCKS ○   OPTIONS ○   FUTURES ○   FOREX ○   AVAILABLE FUNDS ($,¥,£,€):

Time	Buy Sell	Quantity	Name/Symbol	Price	Cost	Proceeds	Net Gain (Loss)	%

TARGET / STOP: R.O.I./R.O.R./R.O.C.:

NOTES

- -

DATE | MARKET CONDITIONS:

STOCKS ○   OPTIONS ○   FUTURES ○   FOREX ○   AVAILABLE FUNDS ($,¥,£,€):

Time	Buy Sell	Quantity	Name/Symbol	Price	Cost	Proceeds	Net Gain (Loss)	%

TARGET / STOP: R.O.I./R.O.R./R.O.C.:

NOTES

DATE

MARKET CONDITIONS:

STOCKS ○ OPTIONS ○ FUTURES ○ FOREX ○

AVAILABLE FUNDS ($,¥,£,€):

Time	Buy Sell	Quantity	Name/Symbol	Price	Cost	Proceeds	Net Gain (Loss)	%

TARGET / STOP:

R.O.I./R.O.R./R.O.C.:

NOTES

DATE

MARKET CONDITIONS:

STOCKS ○ OPTIONS ○ FUTURES ○ FOREX ○

AVAILABLE FUNDS ($,¥,£,€):

Time	Buy Sell	Quantity	Name/Symbol	Price	Cost	Proceeds	Net Gain (Loss)	%

TARGET / STOP:

R.O.I./R.O.R./R.O.C.:

NOTES

DATE

MARKET CONDITIONS:

STOCKS ○ OPTIONS ○ FUTURES ○ FOREX ○

AVAILABLE FUNDS ($,¥,£,€):

Time	Buy Sell	Quantity	Name/Symbol	Price	Cost	Proceeds	Net Gain (Loss)	%

TARGET / STOP:

R.O.I./R.O.R./R.O.C.:

NOTES

· ·

DATE

MARKET CONDITIONS:

STOCKS ○ OPTIONS ○ FUTURES ○ FOREX ○

AVAILABLE FUNDS ($,¥,£,€):

Time	Buy Sell	Quantity	Name/Symbol	Price	Cost	Proceeds	Net Gain (Loss)	%

TARGET / STOP:

R.O.I./R.O.R./R.O.C.:

NOTES

DATE | MARKET CONDITIONS:

STOCKS ○ OPTIONS ○ FUTURES ○ FOREX ○

AVAILABLE FUNDS ($,¥,£,€):

Time	Buy Sell	Quantity	Name/Symbol	Price	Cost	Proceeds	Net Gain (Loss)	%

TARGET / STOP:

R.O.I./R.O.R./R.O.C.:

NOTES

- -

DATE | MARKET CONDITIONS:

STOCKS ○ OPTIONS ○ FUTURES ○ FOREX ○

AVAILABLE FUNDS ($,¥,£,€):

Time	Buy Sell	Quantity	Name/Symbol	Price	Cost	Proceeds	Net Gain (Loss)	%

TARGET / STOP:

R.O.I./R.O.R./R.O.C.:

NOTES

MARKET CONDITIONS:

STOCKS ◯   OPTIONS ◯   FUTURES ◯   FOREX ◯

AVAILABLE FUNDS ($,¥,£,€):

Time	Buy Sell	Quantity	Name/Symbol	Price	Cost	Proceeds	Net Gain (Loss)	%

TARGET / STOP:

R.O.I./R.O.R./R.O.C.:

NOTES

MARKET CONDITIONS:

STOCKS ◯   OPTIONS ◯   FUTURES ◯   FOREX ◯

AVAILABLE FUNDS ($,¥,£,€):

Time	Buy Sell	Quantity	Name/Symbol	Price	Cost	Proceeds	Net Gain (Loss)	%

TARGET / STOP:

R.O.I./R.O.R./R.O.C.:

NOTES

DATE

MARKET CONDITIONS:

STOCKS ○ OPTIONS ○ FUTURES ○ FOREX ○

AVAILABLE FUNDS ($,¥,£,€):

Time	Buy Sell	Quantity	Name/Symbol	Price	Cost	Proceeds	Net Gain (Loss)	%

TARGET / STOP:

R.O.I./R.O.R./R.O.C.:

NOTES

DATE

MARKET CONDITIONS:

STOCKS ○ OPTIONS ○ FUTURES ○ FOREX ○

AVAILABLE FUNDS ($,¥,£,€):

Time	Buy Sell	Quantity	Name/Symbol	Price	Cost	Proceeds	Net Gain (Loss)	%

TARGET / STOP:

R.O.I./R.O.R./R.O.C.:

NOTES

DATE

MARKET CONDITIONS:

STOCKS ◯ OPTIONS ◯ FUTURES ◯ FOREX ◯

AVAILABLE FUNDS ($,¥,£,€):

Time	Buy Sell	Quantity	Name/Symbol	Price	Cost	Proceeds	Net Gain (Loss)	%

TARGET / STOP:

R.O.I./R.O.R./R.O.C.:

NOTES

· ·

DATE

MARKET CONDITIONS:

STOCKS ◯ OPTIONS ◯ FUTURES ◯ FOREX ◯

AVAILABLE FUNDS ($,¥,£,€):

Time	Buy Sell	Quantity	Name/Symbol	Price	Cost	Proceeds	Net Gain (Loss)	%

TARGET / STOP:

R.O.I./R.O.R./R.O.C.:

NOTES

DATE

MARKET CONDITIONS:

STOCKS OPTIONS FUTURES FOREX AVAILABLE FUNDS ($,¥,£,€):

○   ○   ○   ○

Time	Buy Sell	Quantity	Name/Symbol	Price	Cost	Proceeds	Net Gain (Loss)	%

TARGET / STOP: R.O.I./R.O.R./R.O.C.:

NOTES

· ·

DATE

MARKET CONDITIONS:

STOCKS OPTIONS FUTURES FOREX AVAILABLE FUNDS ($,¥,£,€):

○   ○   ○   ○

Time	Buy Sell	Quantity	Name/Symbol	Price	Cost	Proceeds	Net Gain (Loss)	%

TARGET / STOP: R.O.I./R.O.R./R.O.C.:

NOTES

DATE | MARKET CONDITIONS:

STOCKS ◯　　OPTIONS ◯　　FUTURES ◯　　FOREX ◯　　AVAILABLE FUNDS ($,¥,£,€):

Time	Buy Sell	Quantity	Name/Symbol	Price	Cost	Proceeds	Net Gain (Loss)	%

TARGET / STOP: | R.O.I./R.O.R./R.O.C.:

NOTES

· ·

DATE | MARKET CONDITIONS:

STOCKS ◯　　OPTIONS ◯　　FUTURES ◯　　FOREX ◯　　AVAILABLE FUNDS ($,¥,£,€):

Time	Buy Sell	Quantity	Name/Symbol	Price	Cost	Proceeds	Net Gain (Loss)	%

TARGET / STOP: | R.O.I./R.O.R./R.O.C.:

NOTES

DATE

MARKET CONDITIONS:

STOCKS ○ OPTIONS ○ FUTURES ○ FOREX ○   AVAILABLE FUNDS ($,¥,£,€):

Time	Buy Sell	Quantity	Name/Symbol	Price	Cost	Proceeds	Net Gain (Loss)	%

TARGET / STOP: R.O.I./R.O.R./R.O.C.:

NOTES

• •

DATE

MARKET CONDITIONS:

STOCKS ○ OPTIONS ○ FUTURES ○ FOREX ○   AVAILABLE FUNDS ($,¥,£,€):

Time	Buy Sell	Quantity	Name/Symbol	Price	Cost	Proceeds	Net Gain (Loss)	%

TARGET / STOP: R.O.I./R.O.R./R.O.C.:

NOTES

DATE

MARKET CONDITIONS:

STOCKS ○   OPTIONS ○   FUTURES ○   FOREX ○

AVAILABLE FUNDS ($,¥,£,€):

Time	Buy Sell	Quantity	Name/Symbol	Price	Cost	Proceeds	Net Gain (Loss)	%

TARGET / STOP:

R.O.I./R.O.R./R.O.C.:

NOTES

∙ ∙

DATE

MARKET CONDITIONS:

STOCKS ○   OPTIONS ○   FUTURES ○   FOREX ○

AVAILABLE FUNDS ($,¥,£,€):

Time	Buy Sell	Quantity	Name/Symbol	Price	Cost	Proceeds	Net Gain (Loss)	%

TARGET / STOP:

R.O.I./R.O.R./R.O.C.:

NOTES

DATE

MARKET CONDITIONS:

STOCKS ○   OPTIONS ○   FUTURES ○   FOREX ○

AVAILABLE FUNDS ($,¥,£,€):

Time	Buy Sell	Quantity	Name/Symbol	Price	Cost	Proceeds	Net Gain (Loss)	%

TARGET / STOP:

R.O.I./R.O.R./R.O.C.:

NOTES

DATE

MARKET CONDITIONS:

STOCKS ○   OPTIONS ○   FUTURES ○   FOREX ○

AVAILABLE FUNDS ($,¥,£,€):

Time	Buy Sell	Quantity	Name/Symbol	Price	Cost	Proceeds	Net Gain (Loss)	%

TARGET / STOP:

R.O.I./R.O.R./R.O.C.:

NOTES

DATE | MARKET CONDITIONS:

STOCKS ○ OPTIONS ○ FUTURES ○ FOREX ○   AVAILABLE FUNDS ($,¥,£,€):

Time	Buy Sell	Quantity	Name/Symbol	Price	Cost	Proceeds	Net Gain (Loss)	%

TARGET / STOP: | R.O.I./R.O.R./R.O.C.:

NOTES

. . . .

DATE | MARKET CONDITIONS:

STOCKS ○ OPTIONS ○ FUTURES ○ FOREX ○   AVAILABLE FUNDS ($,¥,£,€):

Time	Buy Sell	Quantity	Name/Symbol	Price	Cost	Proceeds	Net Gain (Loss)	%

TARGET / STOP: | R.O.I./R.O.R./R.O.C.:

NOTES

DATE MARKET CONDITIONS:

STOCKS OPTIONS FUTURES FOREX AVAILABLE FUNDS ($,¥,£,€):
○   ○   ○   ○

Time	Buy Sell	Quantity	Name/Symbol	Price	Cost	Proceeds	Net Gain (Loss)	%

TARGET / STOP: R.O.I./R.O.R./R.O.C.:

NOTES

· ·

DATE MARKET CONDITIONS:

STOCKS OPTIONS FUTURES FOREX AVAILABLE FUNDS ($,¥,£,€):
○   ○   ○   ○

Time	Buy Sell	Quantity	Name/Symbol	Price	Cost	Proceeds	Net Gain (Loss)	%

TARGET / STOP: R.O.I./R.O.R./R.O.C.:

NOTES

DATE

MARKET CONDITIONS:

STOCKS ○   OPTIONS ○   FUTURES ○   FOREX ○   AVAILABLE FUNDS ($,¥,£,€):

Time	Buy Sell	Quantity	Name/Symbol	Price	Cost	Proceeds	Net Gain (Loss)	%

TARGET / STOP: R.O.I./R.O.R./R.O.C.:

NOTES

• •

DATE

MARKET CONDITIONS:

STOCKS ○   OPTIONS ○   FUTURES ○   FOREX ○   AVAILABLE FUNDS ($,¥,£,€):

Time	Buy Sell	Quantity	Name/Symbol	Price	Cost	Proceeds	Net Gain (Loss)	%

TARGET / STOP: R.O.I./R.O.R./R.O.C.:

NOTES

DATE

MARKET CONDITIONS:

STOCKS ○   OPTIONS ○   FUTURES ○   FOREX ○

AVAILABLE FUNDS ($,¥,£,€):

Time	Buy Sell	Quantity	Name/Symbol	Price	Cost	Proceeds	Net Gain (Loss)	%

TARGET / STOP:

R.O.I./R.O.R./R.O.C.:

NOTES

· ·

DATE

MARKET CONDITIONS:

STOCKS ○   OPTIONS ○   FUTURES ○   FOREX ○

AVAILABLE FUNDS ($,¥,£,€):

Time	Buy Sell	Quantity	Name/Symbol	Price	Cost	Proceeds	Net Gain (Loss)	%

TARGET / STOP:

R.O.I./R.O.R./R.O.C.:

NOTES

DATE

MARKET CONDITIONS:

STOCKS ◯ OPTIONS ◯ FUTURES ◯ FOREX ◯

AVAILABLE FUNDS ($,¥,£,€):

Time	Buy Sell	Quantity	Name/Symbol	Price	Cost	Proceeds	Net Gain (Loss)	%

TARGET / STOP:

R.O.I./R.O.R./R.O.C.:

NOTES

· ·

DATE

MARKET CONDITIONS:

STOCKS ◯ OPTIONS ◯ FUTURES ◯ FOREX ◯

AVAILABLE FUNDS ($,¥,£,€):

Time	Buy Sell	Quantity	Name/Symbol	Price	Cost	Proceeds	Net Gain (Loss)	%

TARGET / STOP:

R.O.I./R.O.R./R.O.C.:

NOTES

DATE

MARKET CONDITIONS:

STOCKS ⬡ OPTIONS ⬡ FUTURES ⬡ FOREX ⬡

AVAILABLE FUNDS ($,¥,£,€):

Time	Buy Sell	Quantity	Name/Symbol	Price	Cost	Proceeds	Net Gain (Loss)	%

TARGET / STOP:

R.O.I./R.O.R./R.O.C.:

NOTES

• •

DATE

MARKET CONDITIONS:

STOCKS ⬡ OPTIONS ⬡ FUTURES ⬡ FOREX ⬡

AVAILABLE FUNDS ($,¥,£,€):

Time	Buy Sell	Quantity	Name/Symbol	Price	Cost	Proceeds	Net Gain (Loss)	%

TARGET / STOP:

R.O.I./R.O.R./R.O.C.:

NOTES

DATE | MARKET CONDITIONS:

STOCKS ◯ OPTIONS ◯ FUTURES ◯ FOREX ◯   AVAILABLE FUNDS ($,¥,£,€):

Time	Buy Sell	Quantity	Name/Symbol	Price	Cost	Proceeds	Net Gain (Loss)	%

TARGET / STOP: | R.O.I./R.O.R./R.O.C.:

NOTES

DATE | MARKET CONDITIONS:

STOCKS ◯ OPTIONS ◯ FUTURES ◯ FOREX ◯   AVAILABLE FUNDS ($,¥,£,€):

Time	Buy Sell	Quantity	Name/Symbol	Price	Cost	Proceeds	Net Gain (Loss)	%

TARGET / STOP: | R.O.I./R.O.R./R.O.C.:

NOTES

DATE

MARKET CONDITIONS:

STOCKS ○ OPTIONS ○ FUTURES ○ FOREX ○

AVAILABLE FUNDS ($,¥,£,€):

Time	Buy Sell	Quantity	Name/Symbol	Price	Cost	Proceeds	Net Gain (Loss)	%

TARGET / STOP:

R.O.I./R.O.R./R.O.C.:

NOTES

• •

DATE

MARKET CONDITIONS:

STOCKS ○ OPTIONS ○ FUTURES ○ FOREX ○

AVAILABLE FUNDS ($,¥,£,€):

Time	Buy Sell	Quantity	Name/Symbol	Price	Cost	Proceeds	Net Gain (Loss)	%

TARGET / STOP:

R.O.I./R.O.R./R.O.C.:

NOTES

DATE

MARKET CONDITIONS:

STOCKS ◯ OPTIONS ◯ FUTURES ◯ FOREX ◯ AVAILABLE FUNDS ($,¥,£,€):

Time	Buy Sell	Quantity	Name/Symbol	Price	Cost	Proceeds	Net Gain (Loss)	%

TARGET / STOP: R.O.I./R.O.R./R.O.C.:

NOTES

DATE

MARKET CONDITIONS:

STOCKS ◯ OPTIONS ◯ FUTURES ◯ FOREX ◯ AVAILABLE FUNDS ($,¥,£,€):

Time	Buy Sell	Quantity	Name/Symbol	Price	Cost	Proceeds	Net Gain (Loss)	%

TARGET / STOP: R.O.I./R.O.R./R.O.C.:

NOTES

DATE

MARKET CONDITIONS:

STOCKS ○   OPTIONS ○   FUTURES ○   FOREX ○

AVAILABLE FUNDS ($,¥,£,€):

Time	Buy Sell	Quantity	Name/Symbol	Price	Cost	Proceeds	Net Gain (Loss)	%

TARGET / STOP:

R.O.I./R.O.R./R.O.C.:

NOTES

• •

DATE

MARKET CONDITIONS:

STOCKS ○   OPTIONS ○   FUTURES ○   FOREX ○

AVAILABLE FUNDS ($,¥,£,€):

Time	Buy Sell	Quantity	Name/Symbol	Price	Cost	Proceeds	Net Gain (Loss)	%

TARGET / STOP:

R.O.I./R.O.R./R.O.C.:

NOTES

MARKET CONDITIONS:

STOCKS ○ OPTIONS ○ FUTURES ○ FOREX ○

AVAILABLE FUNDS ($,¥,£,€):

Time	Buy Sell	Quantity	Name/Symbol	Price	Cost	Proceeds	Net Gain (Loss)	%

TARGET / STOP:

R.O.I./R.O.R./R.O.C.:

NOTES

•••

DATE

MARKET CONDITIONS:

STOCKS ○ OPTIONS ○ FUTURES ○ FOREX ○

AVAILABLE FUNDS ($,¥,£,€):

Time	Buy Sell	Quantity	Name/Symbol	Price	Cost	Proceeds	Net Gain (Loss)	%

TARGET / STOP:

R.O.I./R.O.R./R.O.C.:

NOTES

DATE

MARKET CONDITIONS:

STOCKS ○   OPTIONS ○   FUTURES ○   FOREX ○   AVAILABLE FUNDS ($,¥,£,€):

Time	Buy Sell	Quantity	Name/Symbol	Price	Cost	Proceeds	Net Gain (Loss)	%

TARGET / STOP: R.O.I./R.O.R./R.O.C.:

NOTES

· ·

DATE

MARKET CONDITIONS:

STOCKS ○   OPTIONS ○   FUTURES ○   FOREX ○   AVAILABLE FUNDS ($,¥,£,€):

Time	Buy Sell	Quantity	Name/Symbol	Price	Cost	Proceeds	Net Gain (Loss)	%

TARGET / STOP: R.O.I./R.O.R./R.O.C.:

NOTES

DATE

MARKET CONDITIONS:

STOCKS ◯　　OPTIONS ◯　　FUTURES ◯　　FOREX ◯

AVAILABLE FUNDS ($,¥,£,€):

Time	Buy Sell	Quantity	Name/Symbol	Price	Cost	Proceeds	Net Gain (Loss)	%

TARGET / STOP:　　　　　　　　　　R.O.I./R.O.R./R.O.C.:

NOTES

DATE

MARKET CONDITIONS:

STOCKS ◯　　OPTIONS ◯　　FUTURES ◯　　FOREX ◯

AVAILABLE FUNDS ($,¥,£,€):

Time	Buy Sell	Quantity	Name/Symbol	Price	Cost	Proceeds	Net Gain (Loss)	%

TARGET / STOP:　　　　　　　　　　R.O.I./R.O.R./R.O.C.:

NOTES

DATE

MARKET CONDITIONS:

STOCKS ○   OPTIONS ○   FUTURES ○   FOREX ○

AVAILABLE FUNDS ($,¥,£,€):

Time	Buy Sell	Quantity	Name/Symbol	Price	Cost	Proceeds	Net Gain (Loss)	%

TARGET / STOP:

R.O.I./R.O.R./R.O.C.:

NOTES

• •

DATE

MARKET CONDITIONS:

STOCKS ○   OPTIONS ○   FUTURES ○   FOREX ○

AVAILABLE FUNDS ($,¥,£,€):

Time	Buy Sell	Quantity	Name/Symbol	Price	Cost	Proceeds	Net Gain (Loss)	%

TARGET / STOP:

R.O.I./R.O.R./R.O.C.:

NOTES

DATE | MARKET CONDITIONS:

STOCKS ○   OPTIONS ○   FUTURES ○   FOREX ○   AVAILABLE FUNDS ($,¥,£,€):

Time	Buy Sell	Quantity	Name/Symbol	Price	Cost	Proceeds	Net Gain (Loss)	%

TARGET / STOP: R.O.I./R.O.R./R.O.C.:

NOTES

· ·

DATE | MARKET CONDITIONS:

STOCKS ○   OPTIONS ○   FUTURES ○   FOREX ○   AVAILABLE FUNDS ($,¥,£,€):

Time	Buy Sell	Quantity	Name/Symbol	Price	Cost	Proceeds	Net Gain (Loss)	%

TARGET / STOP: R.O.I./R.O.R./R.O.C.:

NOTES

DATE

MARKET CONDITIONS:

STOCKS ○ OPTIONS ○ FUTURES ○ FOREX ○ AVAILABLE FUNDS ($,¥,£,€):

Time	Buy Sell	Quantity	Name/Symbol	Price	Cost	Proceeds	Net Gain (Loss)	%

TARGET / STOP: R.O.I./R.O.R./R.O.C.:

NOTES

· ·

DATE

MARKET CONDITIONS:

STOCKS ○ OPTIONS ○ FUTURES ○ FOREX ○ AVAILABLE FUNDS ($,¥,£,€):

Time	Buy Sell	Quantity	Name/Symbol	Price	Cost	Proceeds	Net Gain (Loss)	%

TARGET / STOP: R.O.I./R.O.R./R.O.C.:

NOTES

DATE

MARKET CONDITIONS:

STOCKS ○   OPTIONS ○   FUTURES ○   FOREX ○

AVAILABLE FUNDS ($,¥,£,€):

Time	Buy Sell	Quantity	Name/Symbol	Price	Cost	Proceeds	Net Gain (Loss)	%

TARGET / STOP:

R.O.I./R.O.R./R.O.C.:

NOTES

• •

DATE

MARKET CONDITIONS:

STOCKS ○   OPTIONS ○   FUTURES ○   FOREX ○

AVAILABLE FUNDS ($,¥,£,€):

Time	Buy Sell	Quantity	Name/Symbol	Price	Cost	Proceeds	Net Gain (Loss)	%

TARGET / STOP:

R.O.I./R.O.R./R.O.C.:

NOTES

DATE

MARKET CONDITIONS:

STOCKS ◯   OPTIONS ◯   FUTURES ◯   FOREX ◯

AVAILABLE FUNDS ($,¥,£,€):

Time	Buy Sell	Quantity	Name/Symbol	Price	Cost	Proceeds	Net Gain (Loss)	%

TARGET / STOP:

R.O.I./R.O.R./R.O.C.:

NOTES

- -

DATE

MARKET CONDITIONS:

STOCKS ◯   OPTIONS ◯   FUTURES ◯   FOREX ◯

AVAILABLE FUNDS ($,¥,£,€):

Time	Buy Sell	Quantity	Name/Symbol	Price	Cost	Proceeds	Net Gain (Loss)	%

TARGET / STOP:

R.O.I./R.O.R./R.O.C.:

NOTES

DATE

MARKET CONDITIONS:

STOCKS ○ OPTIONS ○ FUTURES ○ FOREX ○

AVAILABLE FUNDS ($,¥,£,€):

Time	Buy Sell	Quantity	Name/Symbol	Price	Cost	Proceeds	Net Gain (Loss)	%

TARGET / STOP:

R.O.I./R.O.R./R.O.C.:

NOTES

• •

DATE

MARKET CONDITIONS:

STOCKS ○ OPTIONS ○ FUTURES ○ FOREX ○

AVAILABLE FUNDS ($,¥,£,€):

Time	Buy Sell	Quantity	Name/Symbol	Price	Cost	Proceeds	Net Gain (Loss)	%

TARGET / STOP:

R.O.I./R.O.R./R.O.C.:

NOTES

DATE

MARKET CONDITIONS:

STOCKS ◯ OPTIONS ◯ FUTURES ◯ FOREX ◯

AVAILABLE FUNDS ($,¥,£,€):

Time	Buy Sell	Quantity	Name/Symbol	Price	Cost	Proceeds	Net Gain (Loss)	%

TARGET / STOP:

R.O.I./R.O.R./R.O.C.:

NOTES

DATE

MARKET CONDITIONS:

STOCKS ◯ OPTIONS ◯ FUTURES ◯ FOREX ◯

AVAILABLE FUNDS ($,¥,£,€):

Time	Buy Sell	Quantity	Name/Symbol	Price	Cost	Proceeds	Net Gain (Loss)	%

TARGET / STOP:

R.O.I./R.O.R./R.O.C.:

NOTES

DATE

MARKET CONDITIONS:

STOCKS ◯ OPTIONS ◯ FUTURES ◯ FOREX ◯

AVAILABLE FUNDS ($,¥,£,€):

Time	Buy Sell	Quantity	Name/Symbol	Price	Cost	Proceeds	Net Gain (Loss)	%

TARGET / STOP:

R.O.I./R.O.R./R.O.C.:

NOTES

DATE

MARKET CONDITIONS:

STOCKS ◯ OPTIONS ◯ FUTURES ◯ FOREX ◯

AVAILABLE FUNDS ($,¥,£,€):

Time	Buy Sell	Quantity	Name/Symbol	Price	Cost	Proceeds	Net Gain (Loss)	%

TARGET / STOP:

R.O.I./R.O.R./R.O.C.:

NOTES

DATE

MARKET CONDITIONS:

STOCKS ○ OPTIONS ○ FUTURES ○ FOREX ○   AVAILABLE FUNDS ($,¥,£,€):

Time	Buy Sell	Quantity	Name/Symbol	Price	Cost	Proceeds	Net Gain (Loss)	%

TARGET / STOP:

R.O.I./R.O.R./R.O.C.:

NOTES

· ·

DATE

MARKET CONDITIONS:

STOCKS ○ OPTIONS ○ FUTURES ○ FOREX ○   AVAILABLE FUNDS ($,¥,£,€):

Time	Buy Sell	Quantity	Name/Symbol	Price	Cost	Proceeds	Net Gain (Loss)	%

TARGET / STOP:

R.O.I./R.O.R./R.O.C.:

NOTES

DATE

MARKET CONDITIONS:

STOCKS ○   OPTIONS ○   FUTURES ○   FOREX ○   AVAILABLE FUNDS ($,¥,£,€):

Time	Buy Sell	Quantity	Name/Symbol	Price	Cost	Proceeds	Net Gain (Loss)	%

TARGET / STOP:

R.O.I./R.O.R./R.O.C.:

NOTES

· ·

DATE

MARKET CONDITIONS:

STOCKS ○   OPTIONS ○   FUTURES ○   FOREX ○   AVAILABLE FUNDS ($,¥,£,€):

Time	Buy Sell	Quantity	Name/Symbol	Price	Cost	Proceeds	Net Gain (Loss)	%

TARGET / STOP:

R.O.I./R.O.R./R.O.C.:

NOTES

DATE

MARKET CONDITIONS:

STOCKS ○ OPTIONS ○ FUTURES ○ FOREX ○   AVAILABLE FUNDS ($,¥,£,€):

Time	Buy Sell	Quantity	Name/Symbol	Price	Cost	Proceeds	Net Gain (Loss)	%

TARGET / STOP:

R.O.I./R.O.R./R.O.C.:

NOTES

- -

DATE

MARKET CONDITIONS:

STOCKS ○ OPTIONS ○ FUTURES ○ FOREX ○   AVAILABLE FUNDS ($,¥,£,€):

Time	Buy Sell	Quantity	Name/Symbol	Price	Cost	Proceeds	Net Gain (Loss)	%

TARGET / STOP:

R.O.I./R.O.R./R.O.C.:

NOTES

DATE

MARKET CONDITIONS:

STOCKS ◯ OPTIONS ◯ FUTURES ◯ FOREX ◯ AVAILABLE FUNDS ($,¥,£,€):

Time	Buy Sell	Quantity	Name/Symbol	Price	Cost	Proceeds	Net Gain (Loss)	%

TARGET / STOP:

R.O.I./R.O.R./R.O.C.:

NOTES

· ·

DATE

MARKET CONDITIONS:

STOCKS ◯ OPTIONS ◯ FUTURES ◯ FOREX ◯ AVAILABLE FUNDS ($,¥,£,€):

Time	Buy Sell	Quantity	Name/Symbol	Price	Cost	Proceeds	Net Gain (Loss)	%

TARGET / STOP:

R.O.I./R.O.R./R.O.C.:

NOTES

DATE

MARKET CONDITIONS:

STOCKS ○ OPTIONS ○ FUTURES ○ FOREX ○

AVAILABLE FUNDS ($,¥,£,€):

Time	Buy Sell	Quantity	Name/Symbol	Price	Cost	Proceeds	Net Gain (Loss)	%

TARGET / STOP:

R.O.I./R.O.R./R.O.C.:

NOTES

· ·

DATE

MARKET CONDITIONS:

STOCKS ○ OPTIONS ○ FUTURES ○ FOREX ○

AVAILABLE FUNDS ($,¥,£,€):

Time	Buy Sell	Quantity	Name/Symbol	Price	Cost	Proceeds	Net Gain (Loss)	%

TARGET / STOP:

R.O.I./R.O.R./R.O.C.:

NOTES

DATE

MARKET CONDITIONS:

STOCKS ◯   OPTIONS ◯   FUTURES ◯   FOREX ◯

AVAILABLE FUNDS ($,¥,£,€):

Time	Buy Sell	Quantity	Name/Symbol	Price	Cost	Proceeds	Net Gain (Loss)	%

TARGET / STOP:

R.O.I./R.O.R./R.O.C.:

NOTES

• •

DATE

MARKET CONDITIONS:

STOCKS ◯   OPTIONS ◯   FUTURES ◯   FOREX ◯

AVAILABLE FUNDS ($,¥,£,€):

Time	Buy Sell	Quantity	Name/Symbol	Price	Cost	Proceeds	Net Gain (Loss)	%

TARGET / STOP:

R.O.I./R.O.R./R.O.C.:

NOTES

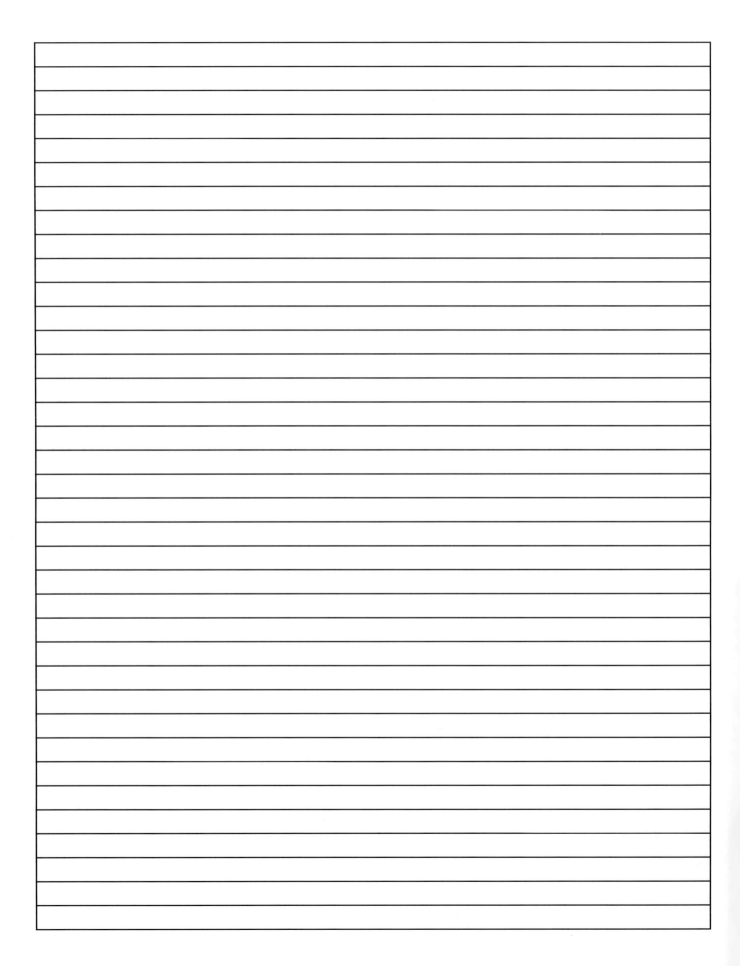

MARKET CONDITIONS:

STOCKS ◯   OPTIONS ◯   FUTURES ◯   FOREX ◯

AVAILABLE FUNDS ($,¥,£,€):

Time	Buy Sell	Quantity	Name/Symbol	Price	Cost	Proceeds	Net Gain (Loss)	%

TARGET / STOP:

R.O.I./R.O.R./R.O.C.:

NOTES

- -

DATE

MARKET CONDITIONS:

STOCKS ◯   OPTIONS ◯   FUTURES ◯   FOREX ◯

AVAILABLE FUNDS ($,¥,£,€):

Time	Buy Sell	Quantity	Name/Symbol	Price	Cost	Proceeds	Net Gain (Loss)	%

TARGET / STOP:

R.O.I./R.O.R./R.O.C.:

NOTES

DATE

MARKET CONDITIONS:

STOCKS ○　OPTIONS ○　FUTURES ○　FOREX ○

AVAILABLE FUNDS ($,¥,£,€):

Time	Buy Sell	Quantity	Name/Symbol	Price	Cost	Proceeds	Net Gain (Loss)	%

TARGET / STOP:

R.O.I./R.O.R./R.O.C.:

NOTES

- -

DATE

MARKET CONDITIONS:

STOCKS ○　OPTIONS ○　FUTURES ○　FOREX ○

AVAILABLE FUNDS ($,¥,£,€):

Time	Buy Sell	Quantity	Name/Symbol	Price	Cost	Proceeds	Net Gain (Loss)	%

TARGET / STOP:

R.O.I./R.O.R./R.O.C.:

NOTES

DATE

MARKET CONDITIONS:

STOCKS ○ OPTIONS ○ FUTURES ○ FOREX ○

AVAILABLE FUNDS ($,¥,£,€):

Time	Buy Sell	Quantity	Name/Symbol	Price	Cost	Proceeds	Net Gain (Loss)	%

TARGET / STOP:

R.O.I./R.O.R./R.O.C.:

NOTES

- -

DATE

MARKET CONDITIONS:

STOCKS ○ OPTIONS ○ FUTURES ○ FOREX ○

AVAILABLE FUNDS ($,¥,£,€):

Time	Buy Sell	Quantity	Name/Symbol	Price	Cost	Proceeds	Net Gain (Loss)	%

TARGET / STOP:

R.O.I./R.O.R./R.O.C.:

NOTES

DATE

MARKET CONDITIONS:

STOCKS ○   OPTIONS ○   FUTURES ○   FOREX ○   AVAILABLE FUNDS ($,¥,£,€):

Time	Buy Sell	Quantity	Name/Symbol	Price	Cost	Proceeds	Net Gain (Loss)	%

TARGET / STOP:

R.O.I./R.O.R./R.O.C.:

NOTES

· ·

DATE

MARKET CONDITIONS:

STOCKS ○   OPTIONS ○   FUTURES ○   FOREX ○   AVAILABLE FUNDS ($,¥,£,€):

Time	Buy Sell	Quantity	Name/Symbol	Price	Cost	Proceeds	Net Gain (Loss)	%

TARGET / STOP:

R.O.I./R.O.R./R.O.C.:

NOTES

DATE | MARKET CONDITIONS:

STOCKS ○ OPTIONS ○ FUTURES ○ FOREX ○ AVAILABLE FUNDS ($,¥,£,€):

Time	Buy Sell	Quantity	Name/Symbol	Price	Cost	Proceeds	Net Gain (Loss)	%

TARGET / STOP: | R.O.I./R.O.R./R.O.C.:

NOTES

• •

DATE | MARKET CONDITIONS:

STOCKS ○ OPTIONS ○ FUTURES ○ FOREX ○ AVAILABLE FUNDS ($,¥,£,€):

Time	Buy Sell	Quantity	Name/Symbol	Price	Cost	Proceeds	Net Gain (Loss)	%

TARGET / STOP: | R.O.I./R.O.R./R.O.C.:

NOTES

DATE

MARKET CONDITIONS:

STOCKS ◯ OPTIONS ◯ FUTURES ◯ FOREX ◯

AVAILABLE FUNDS ($,¥,£,€):

Time	Buy Sell	Quantity	Name/Symbol	Price	Cost	Proceeds	Net Gain (Loss)	%

TARGET / STOP:

R.O.I./R.O.R./R.O.C.:

NOTES

· ·

DATE

MARKET CONDITIONS:

STOCKS ◯ OPTIONS ◯ FUTURES ◯ FOREX ◯

AVAILABLE FUNDS ($,¥,£,€):

Time	Buy Sell	Quantity	Name/Symbol	Price	Cost	Proceeds	Net Gain (Loss)	%

TARGET / STOP:

R.O.I./R.O.R./R.O.C.:

NOTES

DATE

MARKET CONDITIONS:

STOCKS ○   OPTIONS ○   FUTURES ○   FOREX ○

AVAILABLE FUNDS ($,¥,£,€):

Time	Buy Sell	Quantity	Name/Symbol	Price	Cost	Proceeds	Net Gain (Loss)	%

TARGET / STOP:

R.O.I./R.O.R./R.O.C.:

NOTES

· ·

DATE

MARKET CONDITIONS:

STOCKS ○   OPTIONS ○   FUTURES ○   FOREX ○

AVAILABLE FUNDS ($,¥,£,€):

Time	Buy Sell	Quantity	Name/Symbol	Price	Cost	Proceeds	Net Gain (Loss)	%

TARGET / STOP:

R.O.I./R.O.R./R.O.C.:

NOTES

DATE

MARKET CONDITIONS:

STOCKS ○   OPTIONS ○   FUTURES ○   FOREX ○

AVAILABLE FUNDS ($,¥,£,€):

Time	Buy Sell	Quantity	Name/Symbol	Price	Cost	Proceeds	Net Gain (Loss)	%

TARGET / STOP:

R.O.I./R.O.R./R.O.C.:

NOTES

- -

DATE

MARKET CONDITIONS:

STOCKS ○   OPTIONS ○   FUTURES ○   FOREX ○

AVAILABLE FUNDS ($,¥,£,€):

Time	Buy Sell	Quantity	Name/Symbol	Price	Cost	Proceeds	Net Gain (Loss)	%

TARGET / STOP:

R.O.I./R.O.R./R.O.C.:

NOTES

DATE

MARKET CONDITIONS:

STOCKS ○   OPTIONS ○   FUTURES ○   FOREX ○

AVAILABLE FUNDS ($,¥,£,€):

Time	Buy Sell	Quantity	Name/Symbol	Price	Cost	Proceeds	Net Gain (Loss)	%

TARGET / STOP:

R.O.I./R.O.R./R.O.C.:

NOTES

• •

DATE

MARKET CONDITIONS:

STOCKS ○   OPTIONS ○   FUTURES ○   FOREX ○

AVAILABLE FUNDS ($,¥,£,€):

Time	Buy Sell	Quantity	Name/Symbol	Price	Cost	Proceeds	Net Gain (Loss)	%

TARGET / STOP:

R.O.I./R.O.R./R.O.C.:

NOTES

DATE   MARKET CONDITIONS:

STOCKS ◯   OPTIONS ◯   FUTURES ◯   FOREX ◯   AVAILABLE FUNDS ($,¥,£,€):

Time	Buy Sell	Quantity	Name/Symbol	Price	Cost	Proceeds	Net Gain (Loss)	%

TARGET / STOP: R.O.I./R.O.R./R.O.C.:

NOTES

- -

DATE   MARKET CONDITIONS:

STOCKS ◯   OPTIONS ◯   FUTURES ◯   FOREX ◯   AVAILABLE FUNDS ($,¥,£,€):

Time	Buy Sell	Quantity	Name/Symbol	Price	Cost	Proceeds	Net Gain (Loss)	%

TARGET / STOP: R.O.I./R.O.R./R.O.C.:

NOTES

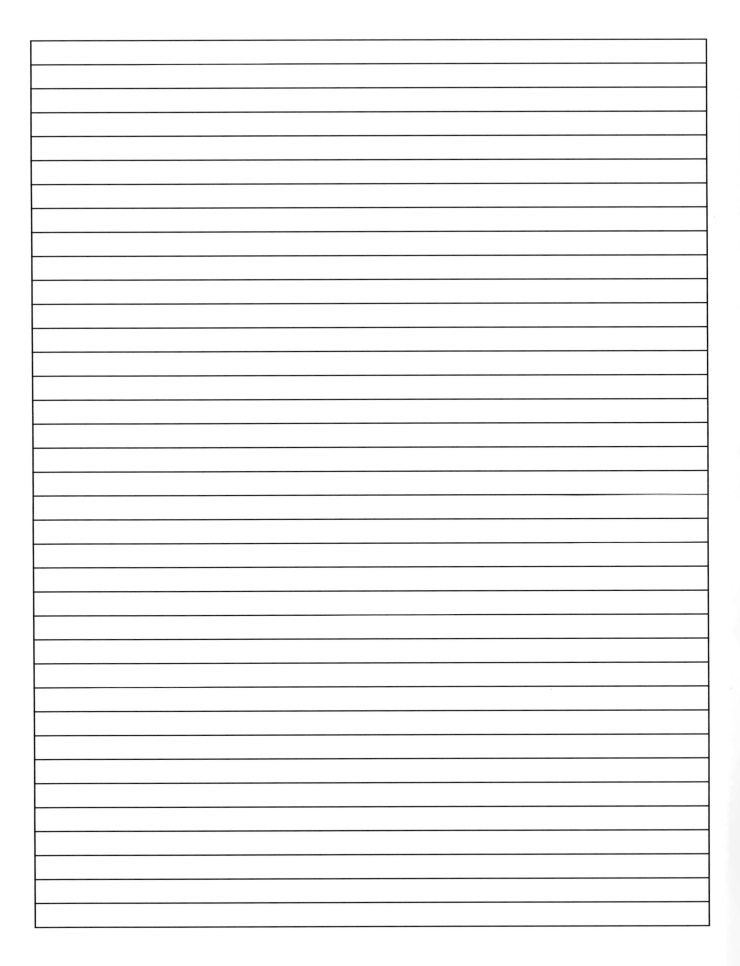

DATE

MARKET CONDITIONS:

STOCKS ○ OPTIONS ○ FUTURES ○ FOREX ○

AVAILABLE FUNDS ($,¥,£,€):

Time	Buy Sell	Quantity	Name/Symbol	Price	Cost	Proceeds	Net Gain (Loss)	%

TARGET / STOP:

R.O.I./R.O.R./R.O.C.:

NOTES

• •

DATE

MARKET CONDITIONS:

STOCKS ○ OPTIONS ○ FUTURES ○ FOREX ○

AVAILABLE FUNDS ($,¥,£,€):

Time	Buy Sell	Quantity	Name/Symbol	Price	Cost	Proceeds	Net Gain (Loss)	%

TARGET / STOP:

R.O.I./R.O.R./R.O.C.:

NOTES

DATE

MARKET CONDITIONS:

STOCKS ◯   OPTIONS ◯   FUTURES ◯   FOREX ◯   AVAILABLE FUNDS ($,¥,£,€):

Time	Buy Sell	Quantity	Name/Symbol	Price	Cost	Proceeds	Net Gain (Loss)	%

TARGET / STOP: R.O.I./R.O.R./R.O.C.:

NOTES

· ·

DATE

MARKET CONDITIONS:

STOCKS ◯   OPTIONS ◯   FUTURES ◯   FOREX ◯   AVAILABLE FUNDS ($,¥,£,€):

Time	Buy Sell	Quantity	Name/Symbol	Price	Cost	Proceeds	Net Gain (Loss)	%

TARGET / STOP: R.O.I./R.O.R./R.O.C.:

NOTES

DATE

MARKET CONDITIONS:

STOCKS ○ OPTIONS ○ FUTURES ○ FOREX ○

AVAILABLE FUNDS ($,¥,£,€):

Time	Buy Sell	Quantity	Name/Symbol	Price	Cost	Proceeds	Net Gain (Loss)	%

TARGET / STOP:

R.O.I./R.O.R./R.O.C.:

NOTES

. . . .

DATE

MARKET CONDITIONS:

STOCKS ○ OPTIONS ○ FUTURES ○ FOREX ○

AVAILABLE FUNDS ($,¥,£,€):

Time	Buy Sell	Quantity	Name/Symbol	Price	Cost	Proceeds	Net Gain (Loss)	%

TARGET / STOP:

R.O.I./R.O.R./R.O.C.:

NOTES

DATE

MARKET CONDITIONS:

STOCKS ○   OPTIONS ○   FUTURES ○   FOREX ○

AVAILABLE FUNDS ($,¥,£,€):

Time	Buy Sell	Quantity	Name/Symbol	Price	Cost	Proceeds	Net Gain (Loss)	%

TARGET / STOP:

R.O.I./R.O.R./R.O.C.:

NOTES

- -

DATE

MARKET CONDITIONS:

STOCKS ○   OPTIONS ○   FUTURES ○   FOREX ○

AVAILABLE FUNDS ($,¥,£,€):

Time	Buy Sell	Quantity	Name/Symbol	Price	Cost	Proceeds	Net Gain (Loss)	%

TARGET / STOP:

R.O.I./R.O.R./R.O.C.:

NOTES

DATE

MARKET CONDITIONS:

STOCKS ○   OPTIONS ○   FUTURES ○   FOREX ○   AVAILABLE FUNDS ($,¥,£,€):

Time	Buy Sell	Quantity	Name/Symbol	Price	Cost	Proceeds	Net Gain (Loss)	%

TARGET / STOP:

R.O.I./R.O.R./R.O.C.:

NOTES

• •

DATE

MARKET CONDITIONS:

STOCKS ○   OPTIONS ○   FUTURES ○   FOREX ○   AVAILABLE FUNDS ($,¥,£,€):

Time	Buy Sell	Quantity	Name/Symbol	Price	Cost	Proceeds	Net Gain (Loss)	%

TARGET / STOP:

R.O.I./R.O.R./R.O.C.:

NOTES

DATE

MARKET CONDITIONS:

STOCKS ○ OPTIONS ○ FUTURES ○ FOREX ○

AVAILABLE FUNDS ($,¥,£,€):

Time	Buy Sell	Quantity	Name/Symbol	Price	Cost	Proceeds	Net Gain (Loss)	%

TARGET / STOP:

R.O.I./R.O.R./R.O.C.:

NOTES

- -

DATE

MARKET CONDITIONS:

STOCKS ○ OPTIONS ○ FUTURES ○ FOREX ○

AVAILABLE FUNDS ($,¥,£,€):

Time	Buy Sell	Quantity	Name/Symbol	Price	Cost	Proceeds	Net Gain (Loss)	%

TARGET / STOP:

R.O.I./R.O.R./R.O.C.:

NOTES

DATE

MARKET CONDITIONS:

STOCKS OPTIONS FUTURES FOREX AVAILABLE FUNDS ($,¥,£,€):
○ ○ ○ ○

Time	Buy Sell	Quantity	Name/Symbol	Price	Cost	Proceeds	Net Gain (Loss)	%

TARGET / STOP: R.O.I./R.O.R./R.O.C.:

NOTES

DATE

MARKET CONDITIONS:

STOCKS OPTIONS FUTURES FOREX AVAILABLE FUNDS ($,¥,£,€):
○ ○ ○ ○

Time	Buy Sell	Quantity	Name/Symbol	Price	Cost	Proceeds	Net Gain (Loss)	%

TARGET / STOP: R.O.I./R.O.R./R.O.C.:

NOTES

DATE

MARKET CONDITIONS:

STOCKS ◯   OPTIONS ◯   FUTURES ◯   FOREX ◯   AVAILABLE FUNDS ($,¥,£,€):

Time	Buy Sell	Quantity	Name/Symbol	Price	Cost	Proceeds	Net Gain (Loss)	%

TARGET / STOP: | R.O.I./R.O.R./R.O.C.:

NOTES

• •

DATE

MARKET CONDITIONS:

STOCKS ◯   OPTIONS ◯   FUTURES ◯   FOREX ◯   AVAILABLE FUNDS ($,¥,£,€):

Time	Buy Sell	Quantity	Name/Symbol	Price	Cost	Proceeds	Net Gain (Loss)	%

TARGET / STOP: | R.O.I./R.O.R./R.O.C.:

NOTES

DATE
MARKET CONDITIONS:

STOCKS ☐   OPTIONS ☐   FUTURES ☐   FOREX ☐   AVAILABLE FUNDS ($,¥,£,€):

Time	Buy Sell	Quantity	Name/Symbol	Price	Cost	Proceeds	Net Gain (Loss)	%

TARGET / STOP: R.O.I./R.O.R./R.O.C.:

NOTES

- -

DATE
MARKET CONDITIONS:

STOCKS ☐   OPTIONS ☐   FUTURES ☐   FOREX ☐   AVAILABLE FUNDS ($,¥,£,€):

Time	Buy Sell	Quantity	Name/Symbol	Price	Cost	Proceeds	Net Gain (Loss)	%

TARGET / STOP: R.O.I./R.O.R./R.O.C.:

NOTES

DATE

MARKET CONDITIONS:

STOCKS ○ OPTIONS ○ FUTURES ○ FOREX ○

AVAILABLE FUNDS ($,¥,£,€):

Time	Buy Sell	Quantity	Name/Symbol	Price	Cost	Proceeds	Net Gain (Loss)	%

TARGET / STOP:

R.O.I./R.O.R./R.O.C.:

NOTES

DATE

MARKET CONDITIONS:

STOCKS ○ OPTIONS ○ FUTURES ○ FOREX ○

AVAILABLE FUNDS ($,¥,£,€):

Time	Buy Sell	Quantity	Name/Symbol	Price	Cost	Proceeds	Net Gain (Loss)	%

TARGET / STOP:

R.O.I./R.O.R./R.O.C.:

NOTES

Tracking

Tracking

Tracking

Tracking

Tracking

Tracking

Tracking

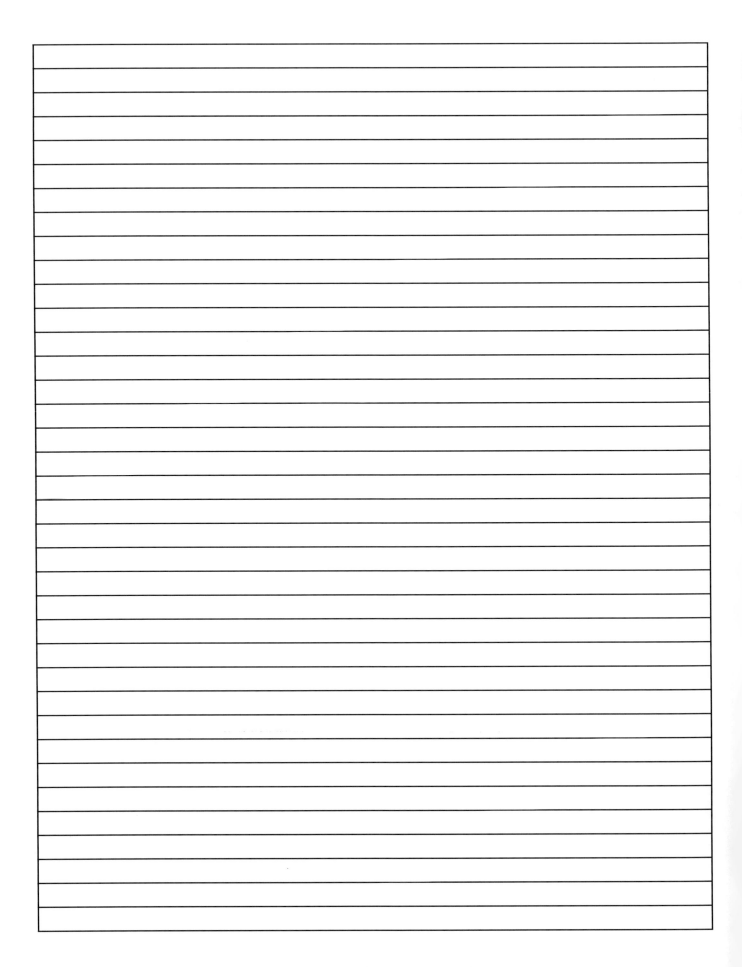

Made in the USA
Monee, IL
21 June 2021